Organizational Climate, Perceived Performance and its Impact

By

Dr. G VENKAT RAO, MHRM, M.Phil, PhD, MBA
Prof. K JOHN, MHRM, PhD
Prof. P ARUN KUMAR, MHRM, PhD

BIOGRAPHY

Dr.GUDIVADA VENKAT RAO, MHRM, M.Phil,PhD, MBA

Dr.Gudivada Venkat Rao(gvr101@rediff.com) has obtained his PhD from Department of Human Resource Management, Andhra University in 2014.Presently he is working as Assistant Professor in HRM, MHRM Programme, Department of HRM, Dr.L.Bullayya P.G.College, Visakhapatnam. He completed his post graduation in MHRM from Andhra University. Previously, he worked as Project Associate and cleared UGC (NET). The Author has 16 publications in reputed National and International Journals and was a guest faculty in Department of HRM, Andhra University. He gave consultancy to reputed organizations in association with senior professors. His area of research interests are Organizational Climate, Unorganized Sector and Strategic Human Resource Management.

Prof.K John, professor in the Department of HRM, Andhra University.
Dr. P Arun Kumar, Associate Professor in the Department of HRM. Andhra University.

Published by TIJ Research Publications PTE. LTD., 51, Goldhill Plaza, Singapore.

ISBN: 978-981-09-8758-9

PREFACE

Organizational Climate is also concerned with the process, style of an organizational life, its content and substance. The organizational climate is an evergreen subject and changes with time. Further, studies on organizational climate and its impact on perceived performance and job satisfaction in a restructured organization in Indian context are incomplete. Therefore, organizational climate in a restructured organization at the unit level is taken up for the study.

The Indian business environment is passing through transition due to growth in world trade and integration of the world market. The shipbuilding industry in India is facing competition. The Hindustan Shipyard Limited is a premier shipbuilding organization on the east coast of India at Visakhapatnam. The consequence of globalization phase in India has reaped profits to some organizations and for some severe crisis. The public sectors worldwide are being restructured through merging with healthy organizations or by infusing funds and by leveraging the inputs.

The Organizational Climate is the summation of perceptions of the individuals. It is the reflection of the individuals" perception on Objectivity and Rationality,

Compensation, Grievance Handling, Working Conditions, Performance Management, Training and Development, Communications, Welfare, Relations and Job Design.

The satisfaction derived by the employee from the job is job satisfaction. The Job satisfaction is an important parameter of measurement for organizational health.

The term perceived performance means the feeling of work experience. The perceived performance is the way one perceives his performance at work. The performance is considered as comprehensive and includes discipline, performance on the job, guidance and counseling for performance, individuality means accomplishing work without dependence and planning and execution of the job on time.

The Chapterisation Scheme for the book was made on the following lines, the first chapter discusses about the theoretical concepts of organizational climate. The book covers approaches and other aspects of organizational climate in detail. Further, the concept of perceived performance was also dealt in length. The second chapter reviews the past and present research in the areas of organizational climate and perceived performance.

The third chapter contains methodology for the present empirical study and further, latest statistical tools which were applied for an in-depth understanding of the inter and intra relationships of the concept. An in depth discussion was presented in the fourth Chapter about the organization, its human resource practices and restructuring of the public sector organization.

The analysis and discussion of the results were presented in the fifth, sixth and seventh chapters. These chapters contain the empirical discussion on organizational climate, perceived performance, job satisfaction and profile factors.

The summary and the conclusion were presented in the final chapter. This book is an abridged version of the PhD thesis entitled "An Critical Analysis of Organizational Climate in a Restructured Public Sector Unit", submitted to Andhra University.

My privileged thanks to Prof.K. John, Prof.P. Devaki Devi and Prof.P. Arun Kumar.

(G.VENKAT RAO)

CONTENTS

Chapter 1

Concepts of

- **Organizational Climate**
- **Job Satisfaction**
- **Perceived Performance**

INTRODUCTION:

The term Organization is defined in the Macmillan dictionary as "to put or bring together, bring into being and create". The word is derived from the Latin word "Organum" meaning to arrange and form[1]. So, organization is understood as coming together of people for common purpose. Mooney and Reiley (1939)[2] say"s organization is a group of people together for common activity, a form of human association for the attainment of a common purpose. But for L. A. Allen (1958)[3] it is the process of identifying and grouping the work to be performed, defining and delegating responsibility and authority and establishing relationships for the purpose of enabling people to work most effectively together in accomplishing objectives. Litterer (1973)[4] viewed the organization as intervening elements between wants and their satisfaction. According to H. G. Hicks and C. R. Gullett (1975)[5] these organizations" may be divided into two, namely as Classical Organizations and Modern Organizations. The Classical Organizations are closed, stable, centralized, authoritative, rigid, and tight with negative environment, whereas the modern organizations are open, dynamic, decentralized, democratic, and participative and have positive work environment. V.S.P. Rao and Narayan Rao (1989)[6] say"s the modern organizations serve a variety of purposes and they are social entities, goal directed, relatively permanent, have structure and are open.

The underlying theory suggests that the organization is;

(i)   Combination of people

(ii)   People have purpose

(iii)   Exhibit group behavior and

(iv)   It is a process

The people join in an organization to fulfill variety of needs and purposes. According to different authors the purpose may be

     (i)   Need fulfilling, goal achieving and to fulfill collective objectives - C. Argyris (1964)[7]

     (ii)   Combination to overcome individual limitation

     - C. I. Barnard (1938)[8]

     (iii)   Enhance capacities through division of work - V.S.P Rao and Narayan Rao(1989)[9] and

     (iv)   Social objectives – Litterer(1973)[10]

The organization may be classified based on some common properties.

Talcott Parson (1960)[11] has classified the organizations into economic organizations, political organizations, integrative organizations and pattern maintenance organizations.

Peter M Blau and Richard Scott (1966)[12] gave four types of organizations viz., mutual benefit associations, business organizations, service organizations and common wheel organizations.

Samul Deep (1978)[13] has propounded that organizations may be classified based on structure, authority, objectives and formality.

According to economic theory, the factors of production are the land, labor, capital and the organization, the returns on these factors are rent for land, wages for labor, and interest for capital and profit for the organization. The Human Resource is a major factor of production in the study of organization. The human behavior in an organization is important. Udai Pareek (1982)[14] defines organizational behavior as interaction of process and these processes operate at macro and micro level in combination and technology, finance, human resources and material are different resources which inter-operate in different combinations.

The human resources are unique and special resources with features comparatively different in psychology. The human behavior is the manifestation of different factors like motivation, attitudes, values, belief, norms and perceptions.

Udai Pareek and T.V. Rao (2006)[15] defines organizational behavior as interdisciplinary behavior science that studies phenomena related to organizations and the dynamics of organization and their various human unit.

Khandwalla (1988)[16] views that organizational behavior is the manifestation of dissatisfaction with the economic theory, principles of management, group dynamics at work, structure and functioning of business organization, rational operating technologies, operation of need theory and alienation at work.

The organizational behavior is studied at different levels, Udai Pareek and

T. V. Rao (2006)[17] suggest that when individual is the organizational unit the concept of motivation, perception, personality, personal effectiveness, decision making, inter-personal styles and attitudes are sources of behavior. When role is the organizational unit, role effectiveness, leadership, work motivation, role stress and coping are sources of behavior in intra-groups. When teams and inter-teams is the organizational unit, team effectiveness, interpersonal communications, conflict management, consensus building and developing collaboration are the concepts which are sources of behavior.

But, when organization is itself the unit, organizational culture, organizational climate, organizational communication, organizational learning, organizational change, organizational development, power, politics and cross-cultures are the concepts analyzed for demarcating the sources of behavior. Whereas when organizational unit is the focus then societal culture, values, positive thinking and learning are sources of behavior.

With leadership style as the basis of behavior, Keith Davis (1975)[18] has propounded four theories of organizational behavior viz., autocratic theory, custodial theory, supportive theory and collegial theory.

Joe Kelly (1987)[19] explained organizational behavior as systematic study of the nature of organizations, how they begin, grow, develop and their effect on individual members, constituent groups, other organizations and larger institutions. Freud (1949)[20] suggests psycho-analytical theory to explain the linkage of psychology with organizational behavior theory. Herbart (1944)[21] explains organizational behavior as a process of learning with emphasis on psychology.

In understanding the subject, there are many approaches to study the behavior of the individuals and the organization. The approach is a systematic path or way for explaining phenomena. The approach is applied to explain the human behavior in the organization. The contingency approach views human behavior as best fit to the organizational requirement (Fiedler (1976)[22]. The human relational approach explains the human behavior as the cause and effect relationship (Elton Mayo (1932)[23], Keith Davies (1975)[24]). The system approach views human behavior as a sub-system, and is inter-related to the system (Chester Barnard (1938)[25].

The environment also influences the human behavior. The environment may be classified as external and internal environment or micro and macro environment. The external environment consists of political factors, economic factors, technological factors, global factors and cultural factors and the internal environment consists of the policy, procedure, objectives and goals.

The above discussion on organizational behavior may be synthesized as follows;

1) Organizational behavior is a process.

2) Interaction between humans happen at different levels and

3) Interaction happens in different combinations.

ORGANISATIONAL CLIMATE:

The organizational climate is often considered as ambiguous term. The above review of theory on organization and behavior invariably reveal the importance of the study on organizational climate. The organizational climate is the most researched topic among the behavioral scientists and it is intensive both at the macro level and micro level. The globalization has intensified the competition. The competitive factor is not confined to product quality but also includes the intangible assets like values, ethics and culture. The importance of organizational climate in the present global context is its ability to provide competitive edge. The global factor has made identity a critical component for competition. The organizational climate is a measure of identity for an organization. Brown and Leigh (1996)[26], Neal and Griffin (1999)[27] identified the organizational climate as the summation of perception which people have about an organization and it identifies the organization.

The problem with organizational climate is the definition. There are many definitions with contrary meanings.

Keith Davies (1975)[28] says it is an assessment of organizational outlook, attitudes, belief, norms, value etc.

Smitha Das (2009)[29] says the organizational climate is the collective personality of a system, characterized by the social and professional inter-action within it. The organizational climate is a personality which enhances positive human relationships, and in turn influenced comprehensively by both the internal and external environments.

Woodman and King (1978) [30] held it may be conceptualized as an attitude at individual, group or organizational level.

James and Jones (1974)[31] claim that two climates exists, one at individual level and the other at organizational level. The individual level variances are characterized as psychological climate and the variances at the organizational level as organizational climate.

Moran and Volkwein (1992)[32] defined organizational climate as a relatively enduring characteristic of an organization which distinguishes it from other organizations and hence; a) embodies members collective perceptions about their organization with respect to such dimensions as autonomy, trust, cohesiveness, support, recognition, innovation and fairness b) produced by member interaction c) serves as a basis for interpreting the situation d) reflects the prevalent norms and attitudes of the organizational culture and e) acts as a source of influence for shaping behavior.

Taguiri.R. and Litwin, G.H.,(1968)[33] urged that organizational climate is the enduring relative quality of the internal environment experienced by members which in turn influences their behavior and can be described in terms of the values of a particular set of characteristics of the organization.

Litwin, G. H. and Stringer, R. A. (1968)[34] defines organizational climate as the perceived attributes of an organization and its sub-systems as reflected in the way the organization deals with its members, groups and issues.

Don Hellriegal and Slocum, J. W. (1974)[35] defines organizational climate as a set of attributes which can be perceived about a particular organization and or its sub-systems by its members. But, for Keith Davis (1975)[36] organizational climate is the totality of its culture, tradition and methods of action of the human environment within which an organization"s employees perform work.

Seyder, R. A. and Benjamin Schneider (1975)[37] defines organizational climate as an experience, common phenomenon and a global expression of the organization.

Litwin, G. H. and Stringer, R. A. (1966)[38] gave a comprehensive definition of organizational climate and claimed it as a set of measurable properties of the work environment , perceived directly or indirectly by the persons who live and work in that environment. But, for Dalton McFarland (1979)[39] organizational climate has profound influence on the outlook , well being and attitudes of organizational members and on their total performance affecting their behavior by defining the stimuli that confronts the individual, placing constraints upon the individual"s freedom of choice and providing source of reward and punishment.

Basing on distinguishable characteristics, Forehand, Glimer, G. A. and B Von Haller (1964)[40] define organizational climate as a set of characteristics that describes the organization and distinguishes it from other organizations as relatively enduring overtime and influences the behavior of the people in the organization.

The organizational climate as action oriented was defined by Georgopoulos (1966)[41] as normative structure of attributes and behavioral standards which provide a basis for interpreting the situations and act as a source of pressure for directing activities. For Friedlander and Margucier (1969)[42], organizational climate is a relatively stable or ongoing property of the organization which may release, channel, facilitate or constrain an organization"s technical as well human resources.

The group perspective approach was used by Taylor J.C., and Bowers (1969)[43] to define organizational climate as the perceived traits of organizational stimuli which become a group property through interpersonal interactions and which modify overt behavior of people within the organization. But for Campbell (1970)[44], it is a set of attributes specific to particular organization that may be induced from the way the organization deals with its members and environment for the individual member within the organization. These attributes give rise to expectancies which may possess either static or dynamic characteristics.

The society is characterized by belief, values, norms and feelings and by using these concepts Payne R L (1976)[45] say"s organizational climate as concept reflects the content and strength of the prevalent values, norms, attitudes, behavior and feelings of the members of a social system which can be operationally measured through the perception of system members or observational and other objective means.

Pritchard R. Karasick (1973)[46] using the influence of policies on internal dynamics defined organizational climate as a relatively enduring quality of an organization"s internal environment distinguishing it from other organizations which results from the behavior and policies of the organization, especially in top management as perceived by the members of the organization. It serves as basis for interpreting the situation and acts as a source of pressure for directing activity.

The climate exists at individual level or organizational level or a group of organizations level, Sharma, B. R. (1986)[47] say"s if the organizational climate is studied at intra organization level with individual as a unit then it is a psychological climate but when summation is done for inter organization comparisons by averaging and when organization is itself the unit the term organizational climate may be used. But, the organizational climate may be viewed as the manifestation of the attitudes of members of the organization towards the organization and it is how they perceive towards the organization.

But, for some it is deemed as a commutation of sub-climates. The individual perceptions of policies, practices and procedure is known as psychological climate and summation of shared perceptions of all these individuals is organizational climate (Pareek (2007)[48], James,L.R.,James,L.A., and Ashe,D.K. (1990)[49],Reichers and Schneider (1990)[50]).

The summated climate for Burke, Borucki, and Hurley (1992)[51] is human relations climate whereas Schneider, White and Paul (1998)[52] regards service climate as sub-system of organizational climate. Brown, and Leigh (1996)[53], Neal and Griffin (1999)[54] has concluded organizational climate like Human Resources Management is an important determinant of organizational effectiveness and productivity. The work performance subsequently is influenced by the individual behavior and Youndt, Snell, Dean and Lepak (1996)[55] predict that organizational climate has an impact on performance and the organizational climate is propelled by the individual behavior.

According to Sharma, B. R. (1986)[56] and Litwin and Stinger (1966)[57] in organizational climate, evaluation is shared by a large number of people within a workplace. Schneider and Barlett (1968)[58] view the organizational climate as both perceptual and an individual attribute.

Rudolphe Durand(2006)[59] feels the human resource practices build the culture of psychological contract of the employee and further , the concept of employee engagement and human resource practices were inter-twined and may be molded for formatting the climate in the organization.

Upasana Aggarwal, Sumita Datta and Shivganesh Bhargava (2007)[60] conclude that in the theory of organizational climate, the level of analysis and comparative climates are the two inconclusive areas.

The above review of definitions view organizational climate as characteristics or attitudes or values which are prevailing in the organization. Further, the manifestations of human resource practices are these characteristics. So, measuring these characteristics with respect to a frame of reference is significant step. The literature is contradictory with authors and researchers suggesting different methods.

ORGANIZATIONAL CLIMATE AND CULTURE:

The organizational climate and culture are the two concepts which attracted the attention of the theoreticians and researchers alike in the recent past. The literature on differentiation between the two terms is contradictory.

Udai Pareek (2007)[61] view culture as a multilevel concept where the first level is values, the second level is climate which is the perception of an organization and the third level is culture.

Mile and Schmuck (1970)[62] and Gellerman (1968)[63] argue that organization culture and climate are same and it is transient. Ostroff C, Kinicki A. J., and Tamkins, M. (2003)[64] differentiated organizational climate and culture and say"s it is the perception of policies, procedures and routines whereas culture explains occurrence of these in the organization. The organizational climate is the outcome of culture. The behavioral aspects are explained by organizational climate and culture is materialistic and symbolic. Cunningham and Cordeiro (2003)[65] claim that culture is a combination of assumptions, values and rules for interactions in the organization. But for Robbins (1984)[66], the organizational culture is a shared meaning about the organization which is distinguishable. The culture reflects the goals, belief and values of the organization and it differs with climate (Decker & Brown (2007)[67] Norton (2005)[68]).

Kouzes and Posner (1993)[69] describes the two terms as organizational climate is met expectations, its temperature, transactual, its tactical and has norms of behavior whereas culture is the nature of expectations , pressure, transformational, strategic, has values and belief.

Keith Davies (1984)[70] differentiates organizational climate as patterns of behavior, attitudes and feeling of the members in the organization while organization culture is much deeper and stable, and the climate is much amenable to change. The organizational culture follows human resources policies and practices. These policies and practices are the builders of culture.

Ostroff, C., Kinicki, A. J., and Tamkins, M. M.(2003)[71] define climate as a perception of organization practices, policies, procedures, and routines while culture conceptualizes with reasons, mechanism and fundamental ideologies and multilevel model integrates culture and climate.

The climate is transient and similar to the moods or feelings of human viz., excitement, anger, fear, optimism or anxiety and it is causative just as internal and external factors for organizational climate. An emotionally variable climate is an expressive person, more open, transparent and understandable person[72].

The above review reveals that both organizational climate and culture are important in understanding the characteristics of an organization. The organizational climate is summing up factors of culture that are perceived within the work environment and results in employee behavior. The shared perceptions and meanings about the culture are passed down the generation. Further, there exists a difference between individual culture and the organizational culture. The above differentiation makes it clear that organization climate follows culture.

APPROACHES TO STUDY ORGANIZATIONAL CLIMATE:

According to Reichers, A. E., and Schneider, B.(1990)[73], there are two approaches for understanding the concept of organizational climate, one is cognitive view where individual representation is the work environment and the other is shared perception of the way things are around.

Bolman and Deal (1991)[74] postulates that a successful organization, utilize a multi - frame thinking for analyzing the organizational climate. The structural frame lays emphasis on impersonal rational decisions to achieve organization goals effectively and efficiently. The human resource frame emphasizes on the individual, the leaders values and harmony within the work environment to achieve organizational goals. The political frame emphasizes on competition and the leaders values, negotiation and compromise to achieve organizational goals. The symbolic frame emphasizes on symbolic leader value, the subjective and strives to achieve organizational goals through interpretative rituals and ceremonies. They recognize that symbols give individuals meaning and provide direction towards achieving organizational purpose.

Mathisen, G.E., & Einarsen, S. (2004)[75] using inter-disciplinary approach explains the linkage between organizational evolution, strategy and organizational climate, with the evolutionary theories in biology – the theories of Lamarck, Darwin and Spencer,

Campbell‟s VSR (variation-selection-retention), and establishes a relationship between biological evolution to organizational conceptualization of culture and climate.

DIMENSIONS OF ORGANISATIONAL CLIMATE:

Litwin and Stringer (1968)[76] analyzed the organization in macro perspective using systems framework, the organizational climate is the perceived attribute. The framework has six motives to understand the organizational climate. The six motives are Achievement, Influence, Control, Extension, Dependency and Affiliation.

Schneider and Barlett (1968)[77] view organizational climate as perceptual as well as an individual attribute, it has following broad dimensions; Involvement, Co-Worker, Cohesion, Supervisor Support, Autonomy, Task Orientation, Work Pressure, Clarity, Managerial Control, Innovation and Physical Comfort.

The organizational climate is the sum of perceptions and a reflection of the interaction between the individual and organization. The organizational climate is a combination of following criteria"s; Innovation, Flexibility, Appreciation and Recognition, Concern for employee well being, Learning and Development, Citizenship and Ethics, Quality Performance, Involvement and Empowerment and Leadership.[78]

Hellriegel and Slocum (1974)[79] feels positive behavior may be built with employee – centered climate. The following criteria constitute the employee – centered climate.

1. Communication: The type of means by which the communication flows.

2. Values: The guiding principles of the organization.

3. Expectations: The expectations of role and decision taken.

4. Norms: The routine way of behavior in the organization.

5. Policies and Rules: The organizational flexibility and restrictions.

6. Programs: The supportive initiatives that define workplace climate.

7. Leadership: The leadership of the organization.

Likert (1967)[80] proposed the following as six dimensions of organizational climate; Leadership, Motivation, Communication, Decisions, Goals and Control.

Udai Pareek (2004)[81] in his explanation says six motives and twelve processes shape the climate of an organization. The twelve processes are Orientation, Interpersonal Relationships, Supervision, Problem Management, Management of Mistakes, Conflict Management, Communication, Decision Making, Trust, Management of Rewards, Risk Taking and Innovation and Change.

The six motives which influence the shape of organizational climate are Achievement, Influence, Control, Extension, Dependency and Affiliation.

George Stern and Carl Steinhoff (1970)[82] has analyzed organizational climate using the following dimensions Abasement – Assurance, Achievement, Adaptability-Defensiveness, Affiliation, Aggression-Blame, Avoidance, Change – Aameness, Conjunctivity – Disjunctively, Counteraction, Deference – Restiveness, Dominance – Tolerance, Ego – Achievement, Emotionality – Placidity, Energy – Passivity, Exhibitionism – Inferiority avoidance, Fantacised – Achievement, Harm avoidance – Risk taking, Humanities – Social science, Impulsiveness- Deliberation, Narcissism, Nurturance, Objectivity – Rejectivity, Order-Disorder, Play – Work, Practicalness – Impracticalness,Reflectivens - Science, Sensuality – Puritanism, Sexuality – Prudishness, Supplication – Autonomy and Understanding.

Taylor and Bowers (1972)[83] in their studies has used the following as dimensions of organizational climate; Technological readiness, Human Resource primacy, Communication Flow, Motivational Conditions and Decision –Making practices.

Jones A and James L (1979)[84] has classified three dimensions for understanding the climate into Job and Role characteristics, Leadership style and Organizational Subsystems.

Halpin and Croft, D (1963)[85] consider the organizational climate as concerned with Disagreement, Hindrance, Espirit, Intimacy, Aloofness, Production Emphasis, Trust and Consideration.

The organizational construct of Lawler E Hall D and Oldham G. (1974)[86] is combination of positive and negative features and it comprises of Competent, Responsible, Practical, Risk-Oriented and Impulsive.

According to Pritchard, R and Karasick, B. (1973)[87] the sub-areas of organizational climate are Autonomy, Conflict vs. Cooperation, Social Relations, Structure, Level of Rewards, Performance - Reward Dependency, Motivation to achieve, Status polarization, Flexibility and innovation, Decision centralization and Supportiveness.

Dieterly, D. and Schneider, B, (1974)[88] made a construct to examine the perceived organizational climate with a measure of Individual autonomy, Position structure, Reward orientation and Consideration.

E.Thomas Moran and J Fredricks Volkwein (1988)[89] through fault line theory explains that negative effects in analysis is better understood by studying the integrative influence, rather than isolating each dimensions. The perceived business performance has four climates, climate for external control, climate for external flexibility, climate for internal control and climate for internal flexibility and ultimately it is related to customer loyalty (Judith S Mac Cormick and Sharon K Parker (2010)[90]. The work – life practices of the organization is critical and influences the structure and culture,

Ellen Ernst Kossek, Suzan Lewis and Leslie B Hammer (2002)[91] propose a linkage between work-life balance and organizational climate.

Andrew Neal, Michael A. West and Malcolm G. Patterson (2004)[92] in their theory on Contingency formulations of Human Resource Management (HRM) suggest that human resources practices and productivity of employees vary in accordance with the prevailing organizational climate and strategic orientation.

Hellreigal and Slocum (1974)[93] view the organizational climate in a simple and static environment as dysfunctional and in a dynamic and complex environment as functional.

Pritchard, R Karsick (1973)[94], Sharma B R (1986)[95] and Forehand, Glimer G A and B Von Haller (1964)[96] view the organizational climate as a measure to distinguish one organization from the other.

The factors of organizational climate namely structure, compensation, communication, working conditions, and culture are the traits of an organization, Moran and Volkwein (1992)[97] feel these may be identified for deficiencies at different levels i.e. individual, group and organization.

The discussion may be summarized on the basis of the above review as

    1) Organizational climate is the collective personality of a system.

    2) It is characterized by the social and professional interactions within it.

    3) The organizational climate is the collective behavior of personality.

    4) Climate is a phenomenon that is influenced by both the internal and external environments.

5) The climate is durable and lasting but it changes over a period of time due to internal and external influences.

Further, Organizational Climate may be studied as

1) Summation or averages of the shared perceptions.

2) Individual perceptions of organizational attributes.

Organizational Climate as concept may be analyzed at different levels namely,

(i)   individual is the unit,

(ii) role is the unit,

(iii)   teams and inter-teams is the unit,

(iv)   organization is itself the unit and

(v)   combination of organizations in an industry as unit.

MANIFESTATION OF ORGANISATIONAL CLIMATE:

The above review of literature clearly states the importance of organizational climate in influencing the behavior of humans in the organization. The intention of any organization is to put its human resources for better use and thereby leverage the organization"s potential. The organization has a strategy to remain competitive in the market; this orientation of an organization is directed to achieve best fit of the human resources. The organization serve number of purposes and satisfy individual, organization and society needs. The individual needs are related to working conditions, compensation, welfare and development. The practices to fulfill these needs are perceived by the human resources and are directed towards outcome. The manifestation of organizational climate is perceived performance, job satisfaction, and job commitment and employee involvement. Sinha J. B.P. (1990)[98] concluded that individuals do not work for bread alone. The manifestation of organizational climate is the attitude, satisfaction, motivation and positive approach and if the organizational climate is the stimuli, then response is the behavior. The organization is a system which is institutionalized with structure, policies, procedures and practices. These practices or set of practices create a unique characteristics as perceived by the members at the unit level, individual level, group of units" level and role level.

Therefore, the corporate and business strategy is oriented by the organization to motivate the human resource in the organization.

JOB SATISFACTION:

The impact of organizational climate is felt at the individual level; job satisfaction is one of such manifestations. And literature is inconclusive and open for research. Andrew DuBrin (1981)[99] defines it as positive emotional predisposition of the individual towards the job and his work. The job satisfaction is explained with the help of needs–satisfaction theories by Maslow (1954)[100], Herzberg (1966)[101] and Alderfer (1972)[102]. The satisfaction with job creates a climate for furthering the performance.

The job satisfaction is a measure of success of the organization (Narain, 1973) [103].

The manifestation of dissatisfaction is industrial unrest, higher attrition rate, absenteeism, alienation, stress and lower performance. The Job satisfaction is important for any organization, the higher satisfaction propel the organization to achieve higher competence. The satisfaction of the individual with job is a comprehensive term and encompasses working conditions, building positive attitude, belief and values, higher productivity, more working man-days and a positive culture. The influence of job satisfaction can be felt on the identity of the individuals, brand image of an organization and the society.

Many definitions were in use to explain the concept of job satisfaction comprehensively.

Hamner (1978)[104] define job satisfaction as intangible, unseen, unobserved variable and a complex assemblage of condition and emotional feelings and such behavioral tendencies.

The definition of Edwin A. Locke (1976)[105] is based on need fulfillment and describes job satisfaction as the pleasurable, emotional state resulting from the perception of one"s job as fulfilling or allowing the fulfillment of one"s important job values, and which are compatible with one"s needs.

Smith P. C. (1960)[106] say"s job satisfaction may be global or specific and it is referred to as overall feeling of satisfaction or the persistent feeling towards the job situation and one"s feelings towards specific dimensions of the work environment.

Need – Fulfillment Theory of Job Satisfaction:

The need fulfillment theory is based on the satisfaction - dissatisfaction dichotomy. The need fulfillment is a rational approach and a gratification of the need results in satisfaction. The non-fulfillment of the needs may result in dissatisfaction. The theory is built on the notion that a satisfied need manifests in better performance and motivate an individual to utilize one"s full potential. The approach provides two models;

1) Subtractive model: This model is based on the premise that non-fulfillment of needs acts as a discrepancy and subtraction acts as negative function on the environment.

2) Multiplicative model: The multiplicative model suggests the needs are multiples of satisfied needs and summation of these is the job satisfaction.

Some of the theories are

Maslow Need Hierarchy : Abraham Maslow[107] has suggested that needs form a hierarchy as physiological needs, safety and security needs, social needs, esteem needs and self-actualization needs. The satisfaction of lower need give rise to next higher level needs; the theory suggests unsolved need manifests in dissatisfaction.

Herzberg's Two Factor Theory[108]: The two factor theory is based on content factors and context factors. The former are hygiene factors and latter the motivating factors. The hygiene factors are inner context factors viz., pay, working conditions, welfare facilities in the absence of these dissatisfaction increases but satisfaction do not increase. The motivating factors are outer context factors viz., rewards, appreciation and new roles, in presence of these satisfaction increases.

Alderfer's ERG Model[109]: The ERG model suggests need hierarchy may be categorized into existence, relatedness and growth. The existence needs include physiological and safety needs, the relatedness belong to social needs and the growth needs are esteem and self-actualization needs.

Vroom Expectancy Theory: Victor Vroom"s[110] theory is a cognitive model based on multiplication. Motivation is a multiple of valence, expectancy and instrumentality. The valences are the preferences people have for outcomes; expectancy is the effort to be put to achieve the desired performance whereas instrumentality is the relationship of performance with reward. The effort is put to achieve the desired result which ultimately is the performance. The perceived performance is achieved through effort to obtain the desired result.

Reference-Group Theory:

The reference group theory suggests the individual takes clue from the group, such group is known as reference group. The individual looks to the group for reference and guidance; they obtain guidance to evaluate the environment. Likert (1961)[111] suggests individual prefer job that meets the expectancy of group.

Katzell, (1964)[112], Locke (1969)[113] suggests that the interaction of percept, need, and value is job satisfaction. These may be translated as actual and expected.

The above literature review reveals that

1. Job satisfaction is inherent to the Organizational climate

2. Job satisfaction varies with respect to Climate.

3. Actual – Expected variation influences Job satisfaction

PERCEIVED PERFORMANCE:

HRM strategy focuses on alignment of vertical and horizontal functions. The vertical alignment is externally focused and horizontal alignment is internally focused (Arthur, 1992)[114].

The horizontal alignment integrates human resources policies and practices towards improving performance. The resource based approach to human resource strategy emphasis on building competencies and motivation to enhance performance (Boxall, P., Purcell, J., & Wright, P. 2007)[115].

The term Perceived Performance is an experience of work as perceived by the individual. Further, the Perceived Performance is a subjective term.

Wright, P.M., McMahan, & McWilliams (1994)[116] using competence approach, defined competence as the behavioral result of conceptions, personal capabilities, motivation, personality, and attitudinal factors. The perceived performance is the perceived outcome of one"s own work experience and it includes behavioral outcome.

The perceived performance is considered as strategic advantage and Jackson and Schuler (1995)[117] consider perceived performance as within the framework of strategic human resource practices and policies.

When human resources practices are aligned with strategy, Balkin and Gomez-Mejia, (1987)[118] conclude they relate to performance. Prince and Lawler, (1986)[119] feels performance appraisal improves appraisal-reward interdependence and it ultimately manifests in performance. The evaluation of performance through appraisal is considered by Meyer et al., (1965)[120] as negative in nature and depending on its use the perception of employees towards performance is built. However, Cleveland et al., (1995)[121] felt the use may be categorized into evaluative function and development function. The evaluative function is for negative use and development function is for positive use. Further, the perceptions on its use influence the satisfaction with performance appraisal. The evaluative-development dichotomy is explained by Ostroff (1993)[122] as evaluative performance is for administrative purpose and perceived performance is for individual development.

Miceli, Jung, Near, and Greenberger, (1991)[123] say"s the performance-reward dichotomy influence the reaction to evaluation, if the dichotomy is weak the perceived outcome will be negative and otherwise positive. The perception of fairness in evaluation depends on the attitude on performance evaluation. Greenberg (1990)[124] concluded that fairness is procedural and this fairness is expected to influence the perception on performance.

Human Resources Management practices influence the performance of employees and according to Shahzad et al., (2008)[125] the phase of development is a determining factor. The phase of development influences the employee performance. Anakwe (2002)[126] suggests that human resource practices in developing countries has been traditional and performance is the criteria.

But, Aguinis (2009)[127] touch upon the behavioral aspects in the definition of performance. Performance is about behavior or what employees do, not about what employees produce or the outcomes of their work. The perceived performance relates with expectancy–reward theory and perceives certain level of outcome for his performance. The behavioral perception of performance is given prominence in the expectancy- reward theory.

Perceived employee performance is the overall belief of the employee about his behavior and contributions in the success of organization. McCloy et al., (1994)[128] has identified the employee performance as a product of three factors namely, declarative knowledge, procedural knowledge and motivation.

Carlson et al., (2006)[129] proposed five human resource management practices that affect performance, these are setting competitive compensation level, training and development, performance appraisal, recruitment package, and maintaining morale. Delaney and Huselid (1996)[130] feel that human resource management systems are associated with superior performance.

Teseema and Soeters (2006)[131] identified eight human resource practices namely recruitment and selection practices, placement practices, training, compensation, employee performance evaluation, promotion, grievance procedure and pension or social security in relation with the perceived performance of employees.

The performance management according to Halachmi (2005)[132] is much more than performance appraisal. The appraisal is systematic measurement whereas performance management is more than measurement. However, Teseema and Soeters (2006)[133] find a relation between performance evaluation and perceived employee performance and further conclude that promotion practices also influence the performance.

The concept of organizational justice is the perception of fairness at the workplace and Greenberg (1987)[134] felt that work performance and job satisfaction are related with the perception on fairness. The work performance is defined by Suliman (2007)[135] as the degree of performance of employee to carry out job in a work setting. Greenberg (2001)[136] based his theory to understand the concept of fairness as perceived in the organization and its influence on work performance as perceived by the employees, further he included norm as one of the influencing factor. Leung and Stephan (2001)[137] has included cross-cultural environment as one of the factor.

Delaney and Huselid"s (1996)[138] furthering the concept of performance capacities say the psychological states on competence create an impact on the performance at the work area. The scale of perceptions of organizational performance or individual performance is subjective. The performance can be a perceptual measure of individual performance or organizational performance.

Thus, the term perceived performance is understood as a perception of work experience and evaluation of one"s own performance at work.

REFERENCES:

1. The Editor (1979), Macmillan Contemporary Dictionary, New York: Macmillan Publishing Company Inc.

2. Mooney, J. D. and Reiley, A. C. (1939), The Principles of Organization, Harper & Bros., pp.1-4.

3. Allen, L. A. (1958), Management and Organization, Tokyo: McGraw Hill, p.58.

4. Litterer, J. A. (1973), The Analysis of Organization, New York: John Wiley, p.9.

5. Hicks, H. G.and Gullett, C. R. (1975), Organizations Theory and Behavior, New York: Mc Graw Hill, pp. 8-12.

6. Rao, V.S.P. and Narayan Rao (1989), Organization Theory and Behaviour, Delhi: Konark Publishers Pvt. Ltd., p.28.

7. Argyris, C. (1964), Integrating the Individual and the Organization, New York: John Wiley and Sons, p.35.

8. Barnard, C. I. (1938), The Function of the Executive, Cambridge Mass: Harvard University Press, p.73.

9. Rao, V.S.P. and Narayan Rao (1989), op.cit. p.37.

10. Litterer, J. A. (1973), op.cit. p.60.

11. Talcott Parson (1960), Structure and Process of Modern Societies, New York: Free Press, pp.42-46.

12. Peter M Blau and Richard Scott (1966), Modern Organizations, London, p.42.

13. Samul Deep (1978), Human Relations in Management, Glencoe Publications: Routledge and Kegan Paul, p.125.

14. Udai Pareek (1982), Survey of Psychological Research in India, 1971-76, Part 1, 2, Bombay: Popular Prakshan.

15. Udai Pareek and T.V. Rao (2006), Changing Teacher Behaviour through Feedback, Hyderabad: ICFAI University Press.

16.Khandwalla, P. N. (1988), Development, A New Role for the Organizational Sciences, New Delhi: Sage.

17. Udai Pareek and Rao T. V. (2006), Changing Teacher Behaviour through Feedback, Hyderabad: ICFAI University Press.

18. Keith Davis (1975), Human Behavior at Work, New Delhi: Tata Mc Graw Hill.

19. Joe Kelly (1987), Organizational Behavior, Delhi: Surjeet Publications, p.483.

20. Freud Sigmund (1949), An Outline of Psychoanalysis, New York: W.W.Norton and Company, p.14. (Translated by J. Strachery).

21.Herbart Simon (1944), "Decision Making and Administrative Organization", Public Administrative Review, p.22.

22. Fiedler (1967), A Theory of Leadership Effectiveness, New York: McGraw Hill Co.

23. Elton Mayo as quoted in F.J.Roethlisberger and W.J.Deiskson, Management and Worker, Cambridge: Harvard University Press, 1946.

24. Keith Davies (1975), Human Behavior at Work, New Delhi: Tata Mc Graw Hill.

25. Chester I. Barnard (1938), The Function of Executive, Cambridge Mass: Harvard University Press, p.9.

26. Brown, S.P., & Leigh, T.W. (1996), "A new look at psychological climate and its relationship to job involvement, effort and performance", Journal of Applied Psychology, 81, pp.358-368.

27. Neal and Griffin (1999), "Developing a Theory of Performance for Human Resource Management", Asia Pacific Journal of Human Resources, 37, pp. 44-59.

28. Keith Davies (1975), Human Behavior at Work, New Delhi: Tata Mc Graw Hill, p.63.

29. Smitha Das (2009), "Organizational Climate - A Performance Enhancing Aspect", ICFAI Journal of Management, No.3.

30. Woodman, R. W., and King, D. C. (1978), "Organizational climate science or folklore?" Academy of Management Review, 3(4), pp. 816-826.

31. James, L.R., and Jones A.P. (1974), "Organizational Climate: A Review of Theory and Research", Psychological Bulletin, 81, December, p.1098.

32. Moran, E. T., and Volkwein, J. F. (1992), "The cultural approach to the formation of organizational climate", Human Relations, 45, pp.19-47.

33. Taguiri, R., and Litwin, G.H. (1968), Organizational Climate: Explorations of a Concept, Boston: Harvard University Press, pp.11-32.

34. Litwin, G.H. and Stringer, R.A. (1968), Motivational Organizational Climate, Cambridge Mass: Harvard University Press.

35. Don Hellriegal and Slocum, John W. (1974), "Organizational Climate: Measures Research and Contingencies", Academy of Management Journal, June, p.277.

36. Keith Davis (1975), op. cit., pp.83-84.

37. Seyder, R.A., and Benjamin Schneider (1975), "Some Relationships between Job Satisfaction and Organizational Climate", Journal of Applied Psychology, No.3, p.318.

38. Litwin, G. H., and Stringer, R. (1966), The Influence of Organizational Climate, Boston: Harvard University Press.

39. Dalton McFarland (1979), Management: Foundations and Practices, New York: Mac Milan Co., p.491.

40. Forehan, Glimer G.A., and Von Haller B. (1964), "Environmental Variation in Studies of Organizational Behavior", Psychological Bulletin, Vol.62, No.6, pp.361-382.

41. Georgopoulos, B. (1965), "Normative Structure Variables and Organizational Behaviour", Human Relations, Vol.18, pp.115-170.

42. Friedlander., and Margulies, N. (1969),"Multiple impacts of organizational climate and individual value system upon job satisfaction", Personnel Psychology, Vol.22, pp.171-183.

43. Taylor J.C., and Bowers (1970), The Survey of Organizations, Ann Arbor, Michigan, Institute for Social Research, Michigan: University of Michigan.

44. Campbell (1970), Managerial Behavior, Performance and Effectiveness, New York: McGraw Hill.

45. Payne, R. F., and Pugh, D. (1976), Organizational structure and climate: in M. D.Dunnette (ed.), Handbook of Industrial and Organizational Psychology, Chicago: Rand McNally.

46. Karasick, K. (1973), "The Effects of Organizational Climate on Managerial Job Performance and Job Satisfaction", Organizational Behavior and Human Performance, Vol. 9, pp. 126-146.

47. Sharma, B. R. (1986), Not by Bread Alone, New Delhi, pp.26-27.

48. Udai Pareek (2007), Understanding Organizational Behaviour, New Delhi: Oxford University Press.

49. James, L.R., James, L.A., and Ashe, D.K. (1990), The meaning of Organizations: An essay In B.Schneider (Ed.), Climate and Culture, San Francisco: Jossey –Bass.

50. Reichers, A. E. and Schneider, B. (1990), Climate and Culture: An Evolution of Constructs", in B.Schneider (Ed.), Organizational Climate and Culture, San Francisco: Jossey-Bass, pp. 40- 84.

51. Burke, M. J., Borucki, C. C., and Hurley, A. E. (1992), "Reconceptualizing Psychological Climate in a Retail Service Environment: A Multiple Stakeholder Perspective", Journal of Applied Psychology, 77, pp. 717-729.

52. Schneider, B., White, S.S., & Paul, M.C. (1998), "Linking service climate and customer perceptions of service quality: Test of a causal model", Journal of Applied Psychology, 83, pp.462- 469.

53. Brown, S.P., & Leigh, T.W. (1996), "A new look at psychological climate and its relationship to job involvement, effort and performance", Journal of Applied Psychology, 81, pp.358-368.

54. Neal, A., and Griffin, M. A. (1999), "Developing a Theory of Performance for Human Resource Management", Asia Pacific Journal of Human Resources, 37, pp. 44-59.

55. Youndt, M. A., Snell, S. A., Dean, J. W., and Lepak, D. P. (1996), "Human Resource Management, Manufacturing Strategy, and Firm Performance", Academy of Management Journal, 39, pp. 836-866.

56. Sharma, B. R. (1986), Not by Bread Alone, New Delhi, pp.26-27.

57. Litwin, G. H., and Stringer, R. (1966), The Influence of Organizational Climate, Boston: Harvard University Press.

58. Schneider, B. (1975), "Organizational Climate: Individual preferences and organizational realities revisited", Journal of Applied Psychology, 60(4), pp.459-465.

59. Rudolphe Durand (2006), Organizational Evolution and Strategic Management, New Delhi: Sage Publications, pp. 190.

60. Upasana Aggarwal, Sumita Datta and Shivganesh Bhargava (2007), "The Relationship between Human Resource Practices, Psychological Contract and Employee Engagement", IIMB Management Review, September, Vol.19, No.3.

61. Udai Pareek (2007), op.cit. pp.33-38.

62. Mile and Schmuck (1980), "Organization Development in Schools: The State of the Art", Review of Educational Research, Spring, Vol.50, No.1, pp.121-183.

63. Gellerman Saul W. (1968), Management By Motivation, New York: American Management Association.

64. Ostroff, C., Kinicki, A. J., and Tamkins, M. (2003), Organizational Culture and Climate, Handbook of Psychology, pp. 565–593.

65. Cunningham, W. C., and P. Cordeiro (2003), Educational administration: A problem-based approach, Boston: Allyn and Bacon.

66. Robbins, S.P., (1984), Organizational Theory, New Jersey: Prentice Hall p.218.

67. Decker, L. E., Decker, V. A., & Brown, P. M. (2007), Diverse partnership for student success,MD Lanham :Rowman & Littlefield Education.

68. Norton, M. S. (2005), Executive leadership for effective administration, Boston, Allyn & Bacon.

69. Kouzes and Posner (1993), Credibility: How leaders gain and lose it, why people demand it? , San Francisco: Jossey-Bass, pp. 40- 84.

70. Davies, K. (1975), op. cit., pp.63.

71. Ostroff, C., Kinicki, A. J., and Tamkins, M. M. (2003), Organizational Culture and Climate, Handbook of Psychology, pp. 565–593.

72. Organizational Culture and Climate: The Personality and Mood of Organizations, as in website http://www.suite101.com/content/organizational-culture-and-climate-a35298#ixzz1IonvaOoZ.

73. Reichers, A. E., and Schneider, B. (1990), Climate and culture: An Evolution of Constructs", in B.Schneider (Ed.), Organizational Climate and Culture, San Francisco: Jossey-Bass, pp. 40- 84.

74. Bolman, L. G., & Deal, T. E. (1991), "Leadership and management effectiveness: A multi-frame, multi-sector analysis", Human Resource Management, 30, pp. 509-534.

75. Mathisen, G.E., & Einarsen, S. (2004), "A Review of Instruments Assessing Creative and Innovative Environments within Organizations", Creativity Research Journal, 16(1), pp. 119-140.

76. Litwin, G. H., and Stringer, R.A. (1968), "Motivation and Organizational Climate", Boston Division of Research, Harvard: Harvard Business School.

77. Schneider, B., and Bartlett, C. (1970), "Individual differences and organizational climate. II: Measurement of organizational climate by the multi-trait, multi-rater matrix", Personnel Psychology, 23, pp. 493-512.

78. Srinivas, Kandula (2007), Human Resource Management in Practice with 300 Models, Techniques and Tools, New Delhi: Prentice Hall of India Private Limited, pp.337-340.

79. Hellriegel, D., and Slocum, J.W. (1974), "Organizational climate: Measures, research and contingencies", Academy of Management Journal, 17(2), pp.255-280.

80. Likert, R. (1967), The Human Organization, New York: McGraw-Hill.

81. Udai Pareek (2004), Understanding Organizational Behavior, New Delhi: Oxford University Press, pp. 650-665.

82. George Stern and Carl Steinhoff (1970), People in Context, London: John Wiley.

83. Taylor, J., and Bowers, D. (1972), Survey of Organizations: A Machine Scored Standardized Questionnaire instrument, Michigan: Michigan University.

84. Jones, A., and James, L. (1979), "Psychological climate: dimensions and relationships of individual and aggregated work environment perception", Organizational Behavior and Human Performance, 23, pp.201-250.

85. Halpin and Croft, D. (1963), The Organizational climate of Schools, Chicago: University of Chicago Press.

86. Lawler, Hall, D., and Oldham, G. (1974), "Organizational climate: relationship to organizational structure, process and performance", Organizational Behavior and Human Performance, 11, pp.139-155.

87. Pritchard, R., and Karasick, B. (1973), "The effects of organizational climate on managerial job performance and job satisfaction", Organizational Behavior and Human Performance, 9, pp.126-146.

88. Dieterly, D., and Schneider, B. (1974), "The effect of Organizational environment on perceived power and climate", Organization Behavior and Human Performance, 11, pp.316-337.

89.Thomas Moran and Fredricks Volkwein J.(1988), Examining Organizational Climate in Institutes of Higher Education, Research in Higher Education , Springer.

90. Sharon K., Parker (2007), "That is my job" How employees' role orientation affects their job performance", Human Relations, vol. 60, no. 3, pp. 403-434.

91. Ellen Ernst Kossek, Suzan Lewis and Leslie B Hammer (2002), "Work–life initiatives and organizational change: Overcoming mixed messages to move from the margin to the mainstream", Human Relations, 4, 63(1).

92. Andrew Neal, Michael A. West and Malcolm G. Patterson (2005), "Do Organizational Climate and Strategic Orientation Moderate the Relationship between Human Resource Management Practices and Productivity?" Journal of Management, August, vol. 31, no. 4, pp.492-512.

93. Hellreigal and Slocum (1974), "Organizational Climate: Measures, Research and Contingencies", Academy of Management Journal, June, p.277.

94. Pritchard, R., and Karasick, B. (1973), "The effects of organizational climate on managerial job performance and job satisfaction", Organizational Behavior and Human Performance, 9, pp. 126-46.

95. Sharma, B. R. (1986), Not by Bread Alone, New Delhi, pp.26-27.

96. Forehand, G. A., and Gilmer, B. (1964), "Environmental variation in studies of Organizational Behavior", Psychological Bulletin, 62, pp.361-382.

97. Thomas Moran and Fredricks Volkwein J. (1988), Examining Organizational Climate in Institutes of Higher Education, Research in Higher Education, Springer.

98. Sinha, J.B.P. (1990),Work Culture in the Indian Context, New Delhi: Sage.

99. Andrew Du Brin (1981), Personnel and Human Resources Management: New York: D.Van Nostrand Co.

100. Maslow (1954), Motivation and Personality, New Delhi: Harper.

101. Herzberg, F. (1966), Work and the Nature of Work, Cleveland: World Publishing.

102. Alderfer, C. (1972), Existence, Relatedness and Growth, New York: Free Press.

103. Narain, L. (1973), Managerial Compensation and Motivation, New Delhi: Oxford & IBM.

104. Hamner (1978), Organizational Behavior: An Applied Psychological Approach, Business Publications, p.216.

105. Edwin A. Locke (1976), "The Nature and Causes of Job Satisfaction" in Marvin D. Punnetteled (ed.), Hand Book of Industrial and Organizational Psychology, Chicago: Rand Mc Nally, p.1342.

106. Smith, P. C., Kendall, L. M., and Hulin, C. L. (1969), The Measurement of Satisfaction in Work and Retirement, Chicago: Rand-McNally.

107. Maslow, A.H. (1943), "A Theory of Human Motivation", Psychological Review, Vol.50, pp.370-396.

108. Herzberg, F. (1966), Work and the Nature of Work, Cleveland: World Publishing.

109. Alderfer, C. (1972), Existence, Relatedness and Growth, New York: Free Press.

110. Vroom, V.H. (1964), Work and Motivation, New York: John Wiley and Sons.

111. Likert (1961), op.cit. p.76.

112. Locke, E. A. (1969), "What is Job Satisfaction," OB and Human Performance, 4, pp. 309-336.

113. Katzell, R. A. (1964), "Personal Values, Job Satisfaction, and Job Behavior" in Borow, H. (ed.), Man in a World of Work, Boston: Houghton Mifflin.

114. Arthur, J. B. (1992), "The link between business strategy and industrial relations systems in American steel mini-mills", Industrial and Labor Relations Review, 45, pp. 488-506.

115. Boxall, P., Purcell, J., & Wright, P. (2007), The goals of HRM, Hand book of Human Resource Management, Oxford: Oxford University Press.

116. Wright, P.M., McMahan, & McWilliams (1994), Human Resources and Sustained Competitive Advantage: A resource based perspective, International Journal of HRM, 5, pp.304-326.

117. Jackson, S. E., & Schuler, R. S. (1995), "Understanding human resource management in the context of organizations and their environments", Annual Review of Psychology, 46, pp. 237–264.

118. Balkin, D. B., & Gomez-Mejia, L.R. (1987), "Toward a contingency theory of compensation strategy", Strategic Management Journal, 8, pp.169-182.

119. Prince, J. B., & Lawler, E. E. (1986), "Does salary discussion hurt the developmental performance appraisal?" Organizational Behavior and Human Resource Decision Processes, 37, pp. 357-375.

120. Meyer et al., (1965), "HRM practices and organizational commitment: Test of a mediation model", Canadian Journal of Administrative Sciences, 17(4), pp. 319-331.

121. Cleveland, J. N., Murphy, K. R., & Williams, R. E. (1989), "Multiple uses of performance appraisal: Prevalence and correlates", Journal of Applied Psychology, 74, pp.130-135.

122. Ostroff, C. (1992), "The relationship between satisfaction, attitudes, and performance: An organizational level analysis", Journal of Applied Psychology, 77, pp. 963-974.

123. Miceli,M.P., Jung, I., Near, J. P., &Greenberger, D. B. (1991), " Predictors and outcomes of reactions to pay-for-performance plans", Journal of Applied Psychology, 76, pp.508-521.

124. Greenberg, J. (1990), "Organizational justice: Yesterday, today, and tomorrow", Journal of Management, 16, pp. 399-432.

125. Khurram Shahzad, Sajid Bashir and Muhammad I Ramay (2008), "Impact of HR Practices on Perceived Performance of University Teachers in Pakistan", International Review of Business Research Papers, Vol. 4 No.2 March, pp.302-315.

126. Anakwe, U.P. (2002), "Human resource management practices in Nigeria: Challenges and insights", International Journal Human Resources Management, 3(7), pp.1042-59.

127. Aguinis, H. (2009), Performance Management, 2nd edition, New Delhi: Prentice Hall.

128. McCloy, R.A., Campel, J.P., Cudeck, R. (1994), "A confirmatory test of a model performance determininents", Journal of Applied Psychology, 79, pp. 493-854.

129. Carlson, D.S., Upton, N., Seaman, S. (2006), "The Impact of Human Resource Practices and Compensation Design on Performance: An Analysis of Family - Owned SMEs", Journal of Small Business Management, 44(4), pp.531- 543.

130. Delaney, J.T., & Huselid, M.A. (1996), "The impact of human resource management practices on perceptions of performance in for profit and non-profit organizations", Academy of Management Journal, 39, pp.949-969.

131. Tessema, M., and Soeters, J. (2006), "Challenges and prospects of HRM in developing countries: testing the HRM-performance link in Eritrean civil service", International Journal of Human Resource Management, 17(1), pp.86-105.

132. Halachmi, A. (2005), "Performance measurement is only one way of managing performance", International Journal of Production Performance Management, 54, pp. 502-516.

133. Tessema, M., and Soeters, J. (2006), op.cit. pp. 86-105.

134. Greenberg, J. (1987), "A taxonomy of organizational justice theories", Academy of Management Review, 12(1), pp. 9-22.

135. Suliman, A. M. T. (2007), "Links between justice, satisfaction and performance in the workplace: A survey in the UAE and Arabic context", Journal of Management Development, 26(4), pp.294-311.

136. Greenberg, J. (2001), The seven loose can (n) ons of organizational justice. In Greenberg, J. and Cropanzano, R. (Ed.), Advances in Organizational Justice, 245-271, Stanford: Stanford University Press.

137. Leung, K., & Stephan, W. G. (2001), Social justice from a cultural perspective. In Matsumoto, D. (Ed.), The handbook of culture and psychology, New York: Oxford University Press, pp. 375-378.

138. Delaney, J.T., & Huselid, M.A. (1996), op. cit. pp. 949-969.

Chapter 2

Present Research in Organizational Climate, Job Satisfaction and Perceived Performance

EMPIRICAL REVIEW:

Organizational Climate is one of the most researched topics the world over; the importance of the topic may be judged from the fact that more than hundreds of studies are being conducted in India. Organizational climate is an important group phenomenon which helps management to understand the perceptions of the members in the organization. But, organizational climate is a contentious issue. The empirical studies give a broad and critical analysis of the studies undertaken on the subject for research. The empirical studies throw evidence on cause and effect relations. The empirical studies prepare agenda for the future. So, in view of the importance of empirical studies, some of the studies related to the topic are reviewed in the following paragraphs.

Stern (1966)[1] in his studies on the relationship between experience and organizational climate found that the freshmen and administrators have higher perceptions on organizational climate than the experienced. Vaid (1968)[2] based on his study on construction workers found that organizational climate is influenced by Adequate Earnings, Job Security, Housing, Opportunity and Work Group. The school climate and its relation to innovation was researched by Bennett (1969)[3] on a sample drawn from high schools in America and found a higher positive relationship in both number and types of innovations in the more open types of climate. The studies of Schneider and Bartlett's (1970)[4] concluded with similar findings in explaining the levels in the hierarchy and organizational climate. Perrow (1970)[5] examined combining samples from various organizations to study the organizational culture and climate with respect to organizational levels and his studies found similar results for all the organizations.

Myers and Kannappan (1970)[6] has concluded that the social and emotional attachment of industrial workers is more oriented towards agricultural life than industrial way of life. Rao and Ganguli (1971)[7] has found Personal Life, Adequate Earning, Opportunity for Advancement, Working Conditions and Policy as the significant factors of organizational climate.

Further, studies by Payne and Mansfield (1973)[8] on organizational climate found variations in climate scores with respect to hierarchy. Johnston (1976)[9] examined multiple climates in organization and found relationship between length of service and climate.

Howe"s (1977)[10] research work finds relation between climate and group membership while examining climate responses on group dynamics, further group membership is a function of climate rather than personal characteristics. Drexler (1977)[11] concentrated on attributes that are specific to organization and which influence variations. But, he found the relationship as weak and the variations with organization effects as minimal. Ansari (1980)[12] also found the variations as low and weak.

Powell and Butterfield (1978)[13] examined the existence of different climates in the organization and found climate differs in the same organization and differs with departments. The same study also concluded that variations may exist within the sub-system climate. The group culture invariably influence the perception an individual holds of an organization, the same results were found by Gregory (1983)[14] in a study on group culture in colleges and universities. In India, Misra (1983)[15] examined the organizational climate and has found Relations, Job Security, Compensation and Suggestions as the major factors.

Austin (1987)[16] made a study on climate and examined the inter relation between organizational climate and independent variables namely, communication, supportiveness and decision making. The study has found collaborative, supportive and conducive environment as the influencing variables whereas the climate is favorable with high morale and satisfaction. Further, he found organizational climate is a construct with several factors and has relationship with job satisfaction, job performance, communication, leadership, structure and commitment. Ansari, Baumgartel, and Sullivan, (1982)[17] and Likert, (1961)[18] has established the same.

Thomas Moran and J Fredricks Volkwein (1988)[19] have found in their studies that climate has relationship with the organizational level and may be used to differentiate one campus from another. They also concluded that administrative sub-units contribute the maximum variance and they have significantly and consistently more positive perceptions of organizational climate than faculty and the latter has comparatively more positive climate with goal clarity and performance standards as intervene variables.

Ruth M. Guzley (1992)[20] has surveyed employees" of a large service organization to determine if individual levels of organizational commitment were related positively to perceptions of organizational climate and of communication climate. The results of the study suggest that employees' perceptions of organizational climate and communication climate were correlated positively with the level of employees' organizational commitment.

Cheryl L. Maranto, Andrea E.C. Griffin (1993)[21] has examined fairness, gender equity and found existence of chilly climate for women. They perceive existence of procedural fairness and gender equity but feel excluded and low in representation.

Agrawal, N.M.(1993)[22] concentrated his studies on the need for creating strong work cultures for developing organizational climate for high performance work organizations. According to him, restructuring through formation of autonomous work groups, reducing hierarchies, relocation, creating awareness about the existing work culture and acculturation are some of the processes by which a strong work culture can be developed.

Vijaya and Srinivasan (1996)[23] has concluded in their studies that better understanding can be maintained in the organization through effectively managing psychological climate. Venkateswaran and Ananthraman (1996)[24] in their study on accidents in Banks found existence of positive and negative climatic perceptions. The Human Resource Development Climate was found to be critical for the success of training and development initiatives in a study conducted by Biswas (1998).[25]

Mark A. Shadur, Rene Kienzle, John J. Rodwell (1999)[26] based on their study, predicted that organizational climate influences employees" perceptions of involvement. Further, participation in decision making, teamwork, and communication are the essential ingredients of employee involvement. The results significantly predicted that organizational climate play a supportive role in motivating employee towards involvement. Employee demographic data, employee affective attitudes (job satisfaction, commitment, and stress), and three dimensions of organizational climate (bureaucracy, innovation, and support) were the classifications used to study the interrelationship.

Hoy and Miskel (2001)[27] in their study, found both task oriented and relations oriented style as effective in a healthy school climate with dynamic leadership.

Abinash Panda and Gupta, R. K. (2002)[28] has used three perspectives differentiated, fragmented and integrated framework to understand the organizational culture and climate. The study found it as „differentiated" and „fragmented", though the management feels it has a strong „integrated" culture.

Agarwal, M. and Bose, Sudeepa (2004)[29] examined the relationship between procedural justice, climate and role efficacy in public and private sector in Indian organizations. The study found across all forms of organizations, fairness in implementing human resource decisions is an intervening variable in management's attempt to develop the role efficacy of members. The creation of positive work environment climate is dependent on members" perception of fairness in decision making. Further, the study concluded that fairness in human resources practices significantly influence a climate which provides support for innovation, enables the environment with trust between the superior and the subordinate and for members" participation in decision- making.

Kirk L. Rogg, David B. Schmidt, Carla Shull and Neal Schmitt (2005)[30] concluded that organizational climate influences the relationship between human resource practices and customer satisfaction. The human resource practices were found as influencing factors on organizational outcomes.

Andrew Neal, Michael A. West and Malcolm G. Patterson (2005)[31] made a detailed study by using longitudinal design based on multi-source data. The study found, a positive organizational climate with internal and external best-fit will influence the relationship between human resource management practices and productivity. But, under the same circumstances based on Resources based view the study also found that the relationship between human resource management practices and productivity was higher even when organizational climate is poor. The researchers concluded that the availability of time is the factor which influences the increase in productivity.

Further, linkage between organizational climate variables like employees" perception towards organizations commitment to welfare, supportive leadership and productivity was found in the study.

McDuffie (1995)[32] found variable relationship between organizational climate variables (participation, autonomy and welfare) and high quality HRM practices in the environment of best fit.

Wynn and Carboni (2006)[33] report that teachers are more likely to remain in the profession when they are satisfied with the leadership and with the climate.

The relationship of individual-level climate perceptions and organizational climate with job satisfaction was examined by Schulte, M., Ostroff, C. and Kinicki, A. J. (2006)[34]. The study found that in a given work environment, the climate is significantly influenced with individual attitudes, and after taking individuals" non-consistent perceptions of the climate into account the results were same.

Richard E. Stup, (2006)[35] study has found that good communications are critical for effective work environment climate and performance feedback is vital to such communication. Further, a stable work climate helps in building high performing workforce.

Schulte, M., Ostroff, C. and Kinicki, A. J. (2006)[36] have concluded through their studies that job satisfaction is significantly related with both individual-level climate perceptions and organizational climate. The climate was examined at two levels individual level and unit level. The analysis found individual perception of climate made a major impact as percentage of variance in individuals" satisfaction. The overall climate in an organization show influence on individual attitudes and perceptions.

Avinash Kumar Srivastav (2007)[37] has conducted studies in telecommunication equipment manufacturing unit in the public sector. The results found no correlation between the three variables viz., achievement climate, role stress and coping strategy. But, achievement climate is related to coping strategy in the Research and Development and Production functions, and to role stress in quality and miscellaneous functions.

Graeme Currie and Andy Lockett (2007)[38] made a study on transformational leadership and climate within public service organizations in England. The results show that internal factors for leadership change influence the climate.

King, E. B., De Chermont, K., West, M., Dawson, J. F. and Hebl, M. R. (2007)[39], assumed that climate theories and practioners" create an enabling climate for the employees. Further, their studies in health care organizations predicted and found that organizational climate for innovation removed or minimized the negative effects of work demands on organizational performance.

Hui, C. H., Chiu, W. C. K., Yu, P. L. H., Cheng, K. and Tse, H. H. M. (2007)[40] studies suggest that the employee service quality was low when both the service climate and the supervisor's leadership behavior were lacking. When the service climate was unfavorable, effective leadership behavior played a compensatory role in maintaining performance standards towards external customers. When the leadership was ineffective, a favorable service climate compensated for the negative effect on service quality to internal customers.

Gonzalez-Roma, V., Fortes-Ferreira, L. and Peiro, J. M. (2009)[41] find that only strong climates are related to financial team performance over time.

Judith S McCormick, Sharon K Parker (2010)[42] on analysis of their data held that climates influence business performance. The climate as dependent variable is affected by customer loyalty moderated with control, external and internal flexibility. Further, the climate manifestation is perceived business performance and the climate is directly proportional to effectiveness.

Alison M. Konrad, Kathleen Cannings, Caren B. Goldberg (2010)[43] has examined the gender influences on organizational climate. The findings of the research show women who worked in medical units with a larger percentage of men or under male supervisor or with a male head reported more gender harassment and discrimination. The findings show a relationship between gender, psychological climate and organizational climate. Michael D. Thompson (2009)[44] findings reveal that the independent organizational climate variables such as supportive culture, worker autonomy, advancement and professional relationships with superiors and subordinates exert influence on satisfaction. The organizational climate determines and varies with perceptions on human resources practices.

Soumendu Biswas (2010)[45] concludes that the psychological climate of the workplace is viewed as one of the most important environmental factors affecting an individual's workplace attitudes. Further, affective commitment plays a moderator role between psychological climate and organizational citizenship behavior.

Halpin and Croft (1963) [46], concentrated mainly on relationships and climate. The relationship among group members and the relationship between management and teaching staff are invariably influencing the organizational climate.

Job Satisfaction has been subjected to intense study by many researchers. The study has mainly revolved around

    i.   what constitute job satisfaction

    ii.   sources of job satisfaction

    iii.   influencers of job satisfaction

    iv.   relationship with profile factors and

    v.   relationship with organizational climate.

Hoppock (1935)[47] in their earlier studies reported existence of positive correlation between organizational levels and job satisfaction and the same was found in studies conducted by Centers (1948)[48].

Walker and Guest (1952)[49] studies reveal that people prefer to work in groups and satisfaction is high among people working in groups than in isolated work sites.

Trow (1957)[50] and Sanford (1950)[51] researched on the relationship between leadership styles and satisfaction, their studies found that the supervision by high status and strong leaders satisfy authoritarian subordinates.

Fred Luthans (1981)[52] works on satisfaction shows evidence that supervisors style of participatory functioning effects workers satisfaction with climate, further extent of participation in decision making process has a lesser effect on satisfaction.

Herzberg (1957)[53], based on review of literature on job satisfaction in depth, concluded that the morale and job satisfaction increases with increase in the levels of occupations.

Porter (1961)[54] focused his study on need-fulfillment deficiency in the lower and middle management levels. The results reveal that the vertical location of management positions appears to be an important variable in determining the extent to which psychological needs are fulfilled. Further, esteem, autonomy, and self-actualization needs were significantly more satisfied in the middle than in the lower management levels.

Guha (1965)[55] has found that the demographic and identity variables are positively and significantly related with satisfaction especially the age and designation.

Palmore (1969)[56] found evidence through a research conducted and concluded that the people who like work are likely to live longer. The people with greater satisfaction enjoy life more than dissatisfied people . The dissatisfaction effects health.

Perrow (1970)[57] examined samples by combining various organizations, and then he applied various tests to find the relationship of organizational levels with organizational culture and climate. Since organizations differ widely, he concluded that the result may be either exceedingly general or very trivial.

Armstrong (1971)[58] found in a study of engineers and assemblers no support for the dichotomy in motivation factors, though content factors made the greatest contribution to overall job satisfaction regardless of the level.

Starcevjch's (1972)[59] study on first line supervisors, middle managers, and professional employees found organizational level did not significantly affect the judged order of importance of job factors for either job satisfaction or job dissatisfaction.

Narain (1973)[60] recognized that personal growth accomplishment and recognition increased with increasing levels of hierarchy and found that security was given more importance. The personal growth, accomplishment, recognition and security showed a linear relationship with organizational levels. Further, the task variables and responsibility showed high level association and greatly contributed to job satisfaction.

Singh and Srivastava, (1975)[61] found positive correlation between organizational levels and job satisfaction among the Indian supervisors and rank and file workers.

Mirza S. Saiyadain (1977)[62] has probed the relationship between the organizational levels and job satisfaction, the relationship was examined keeping some assumptions as constants. The result was found to be homogenous at all levels except social.

Baldev R., Sharma (1980)[63] conducted research on job satisfaction as the dependent variable and monthly income, work technology, occupational aspirations, recruitment policy and union involvement as independent variables. The result conforms with Herzberg"s two factor theory, monetary benefits was not an important explanatory factor but work technology, recruitment policy and union involvement were found to be affecting job satisfaction outcome.

R D Sharma and Jeevan Jyoti (2006)[64] examined the relationship between job satisfaction and different factors, within school teachers. The principal"s behavior, society and colleagues" behavior, work itself, pay and rewards, growth opportunities and recognition, and students" behavior and others influenced job satisfaction. Further, the study has found that the secondary level teachers are more satisfied than primary level teachers. In comparison with government teachers, the study found private teachers are more satisfied and it is attributed to the pay package and lack of friendly atmosphere in the private schools. The study found level of education and gender affects the level of satisfaction.

Fred Luthans (1981) [65] felt workers do not take working conditions as a factor affecting them unless they are very bad.

Solomon E (1996)[66] study pointed out the need for restricting of reward system, application of goal setting and job redesigning as the factors affecting the organizational climate and job satisfaction.

Sharon K. Parker (2007)[67] based on two empirical studies concluded that the behavior is influenced by the role definition and its orientation, which in turn determines performance. The first study revealed variations in performance is linked to flexible role in its assessments. The second study showed flexible role orientation with high autonomy self-efficacy, locus of control, and job aspiration influence variations in performance.

Padmaja Palekar (2007)[68] conducted research on high autonomy jobs and low autonomy jobs. In both studies, role orientation predicted performance more strongly than other work attitudes and including job satisfaction. And also found that organizational background variables such as age, size and turnover serve as important factors in analyzing the impact of strategic human resource management on human resources practices, performance and climate.

Celio AA Sousa ,Willem F de Nijs ,Paul HJ Hendriks (2010)[69] made a study on implementation of performance systems in services. The role ambivalence is viewed as impediments of performance and it is both problematic and challenging.

Sushmita Srivastava (2011)[70] suggests significant relationship between role clarity, perceived planned job change and perceived work place support on perceived job performance. The absence of perceived workplace support has a substantial negative impact on perceived performance.

Venkat Rao,Gudivada and Devaki Devi,P.(2012)[71] in an independent study conducted in 10 public sector and 8 private sector industrial establishments has found that the performance level of the employees is lesser than their job satisfaction. Christina R and Dr.A. Umesh Samuel Jebuseelam (2012)[72] held that when employees internalize HRD values, there will emerge a conducive climate. The above findings were based on the research work conducted by them on HRM and climate.

The influence of transformational leadership on organizational climate was found to diminish due to backward influence by Meera Shankar and Omer Bin Sayeed (2012)[73] in their study. Here, Trusting Relationship, Team-Orientedness, Goal Setting freedom and organizational power direction were exerting influence on leader and ultimately the climate.

The organizational culture with the following dimensions namely leadership, structure, innovation, job performance, appraisal, planning and communication support learning organization and it in turn succeeds in giving business excellence, Ashish Sinha and Bindu Arora (2012)[74] has proved it in their study.

Davar, S.C., and Ranji Bala(2012)[75] based on their study concludes that moderator variables like occupational type,studies and scale of measurement affect the magnitude of relationship between satisfaction and performance.

According to Boh,Wai Fong and Wong,Sze Sze(2013) the usefulness of knowledge sharing mechanism namely informal personalization, formal codification and formal personalization depends on perceptions of organizational climate and managers" effectiveness. They study reveals that warm and cooperative climate influences individuals perception of all the three types of Knowledge Sharing Mechanism"s, in competitive climate individuals preferences for formal codification and personalization increases. However, the individuals are supportive when they perceive their managers are more effective. This study links the importance of organizational climate and individual"s preference for knowledge support mechanisms.

Wang, J.L., Zhang, D.J. and Jackson, L. A. (2013)[77] made a study to examine the effects of locus of control, self-esteem, and organizational climate on psychological empowerment among Chinese teachers. This study finds positive relationship of self-esteem and organizational climate factors namely, professional growth, decision making, appraisal and recognition, supportive leadership and communication with psychological empowerment. However, locus of control has no predictive effect on psychological empowerment.

Arun Kumar(2002)[78] in his studies on coal workers has observed strong relationship between organizational climate and other factors like satisfaction, motivation and morale. In that study extent of unionization was also observed and was influencing the organizational climate.

GAPS IN THE PRESENT LITERATURE:

The Organizational Climate is the most researched topic in the present day global environment. The strategic orientation towards change made environment more dynamic in the present business context. The Blue Ocean Group suggests that environment and structure of the organization either influence each other or both[79].

The organizational climate can be studied at two levels;

1) Organization as a unit or

2) Industry as a unit

The above review of literature brings out the significance of the organizational climate and its importance to the organization, the manifestation of organizational climate is manifold. The organizational climate is differentiated from culture by some researchers while others find no differentiation. Further, the organizational climate is the perceived outcome of organization in action. The perceived outcome of the actions is again a combination of different dimensions while discussion still goes on whether organizational climate is the sum of the factors or to be studied in isolation. The effectiveness of the organizational policies, programmes and practices are the way the people in the organization perceive towards them. But, the way they perceive is organizational climate. In view of its significance, organizations give more importance to study organization climate frequently. The organizational climate is a combination of different factors; the authors differ in opinion regarding the number of factors, content of factors and combination of the factors.

Many authors has differentiated climate as two 1) psychological climate and 2) organizational climate. Udai Pareek (2007)[80] uses the percepts of the above two to understand the working of organizational climate in organizations. The Human Resources Management is set of practices, these practices have bundle of choices. The strategic human resources management envisages choosing the alternative with best fit and its perceived manifestation is organizational climate. The above literature clearly brings out the distinctions. The empirical studies show some kind of relationship between organizational climate outcome and human resources practices. But the studies are incomplete since environmental factors differ. The environmental factors create different situations. Human resources management is not immune to environmental effects; therefore a need is there to study human resources practices relationship with organizational climate. The Human Resources practices namely human resources flow, reward system, work flow etc., are the sub-systems within the system and were tested for their relationship with organizational climate by the previous studies, but the above literature and empirical review suggests that some areas remained untouched or incomplete and those aspects on which results were showed is ambiguous, inconclusive or require further studies. Therefore, much scope exists for further research.

The industry wise studies show different patterns, the empirical studies were concentrated mainly in the manufacturing sector. Some foreign research works exists in manufacturing sector. The Indian Business environment is completely different from the global environment; the latest trend in Indian business environment is culture building. The above empirical review suggests as culture changes organizational climate is bound to change. The organizational climate is not constant and with time period any change in practice is likely to influence it, therefore organizational climate survey is to be done regularly. The importance of organizational climate in the present context of globalization is enormous. In India, there are empirical reviews on organizational climate in manufacturing and service both in public and private sectors but these are inconclusive. The organizational climate dimensions namely Objectivity and Rationality, Compensation, Grievance Handling, Working Conditions, Performance Management, Training and Development, Communications, Welfare, Relations and Job Design were to some extent examined by different researchers. The Objectivity and Rationality comprises of rational policies and it impacts the organizational climate, Baldev Sharma (1980)[81] has established the relationship in his studies on eight manufacturing industries. His studies in addition to the previous studies include scope for advancement, monetary benefits, participative management, recognition and appreciation and job nature and security.

The empirical review suggests different researchers had adopted different dimensions in the summation, but, uniformity was not found in many of the studies. Thus, the constitution of dimensions is an interesting aspect for research on organizational climate. The measures based on perception are prone to variance; Delaney &

Huselid"s (1996)[82] adopted the perceptual measures to study the impact of human resources management practices on organizational performance. The study based on combining the samples to large extent show the organizational climate (Perrow, 1950)[83].

The importance of organizational climate to the organization is clearly established in the empirical studies. The manifestation of the organizational climate is job satisfaction and perceived performance. The dimension wise influence on organizational climate, job satisfaction and perceived performance is subject matter for further research both inter and intra as the empirical studies show that in dynamic environment, dimensions are not constant, environment is variable and the human resources practices are bound to change. Therefore, the extent of variable influence on organizational climate and its manifested forms require in-depth analysis. As pointed out earlier, sector wise studies are also limited. In India, the studies are concentrated mainly in manufacturing and service sectors. In post globalization phase merger, acquisition, takeovers, transfer and restructuring are common. In India, government owned public sector face intensive competition from dynamic private sector. The protective shield around public sector is removed and more autonomy is granted. But, some of the public sector organizations with accumulated losses failed to face competition. The government policy in such situation is disinvestment, privatization or restructuring. The restructuring is the process of making the organization viable through financial and human resources leveraging. The studies on organizational climate in such restructured organization are essential to frame the organizational policies. Therefore, a need is there to do further research in the following below mentioned areas.

1. Constituent dimensions of organizational climate.

2. Organizational climate in single organization.

3. Organizational climate in multiple organizations in a single Industry.

4. Organizational climate in merged, transferred, restructured and turnaround organizations.

REFERENCES:

1.　Stern Stem, G. (1966), Myth and reality in the American college, AUP Bulletin, Winter.

2.　Vaid, K.N., As quoted in Saiyadian, M.S., Human Resources Management, New Delhi: Tata McGraw Hill, 1988.

3. Bennett, R. E. (1969), An analysis of the relationships of organizational climate to innovations in selected schools of Pennsylvania and New York, Dissertation Abstracts, 30, 942A.

4. Schneider, B., and Bartlett, C. (1970), "Individual differences and organizational climate. II: Measurement of organizational climate by the multi-trait, multi-rater matrix", Personnel Psychology, 23, pp.493-512.

5. Perrow, C. (1970), Organizational Analysis: A Sociological View,
Belmont: Wadsworth.

6. Myers and Kannappan (1970), Industrial Relations in India, Bombay: Asia Publishing House, p.87.

7. Rao and Ganguli (1971), As quoted in Saiyadian, M.S.,Human Resources Management, New Delhi: Tata McGraw Hill.

8. Payne, R. L., and Mansfield, R. (1973), "Relationships of perceptions of Organizational Climate to organizational structure, context, and hierarchal context, and hierarchal position", Administrative Science Quarterly, 18, pp. 515-526.

9.　Johnston, H.R. (1976), "A new conceptualization of source of organizational climate", Administrative Science Quarterly, 21, pp. 95-103.

10. Howe, J. G. (1977), "Group climate: An exploratory analysis of construct validity", Organizational Behavior and Human Performance, 19, pp. 106-125.

11. Drexler (1977), "Organizational climate: Its homogeneity within organizations", Journal of Applied Psychology, 62(1), pp.38-42.

12. Ansari (1980), Organizational climate: Homogeneity within and heterogeneity between organizations, Social and Economic Studies III (1), pp.89-96.

13. Powell, G. N., and Butteffield, D. A. (1978), "The oase for subsystem climates in organizations", Academy of Management Review, 3, pp.151-157.

14. Gregory (1983), "Native-view paradigms: Multiple cultures and culture conflicts in organizations", Administrative Science Quarterly, 28(3), p. 359.

15. Misra (1983), As quoted in Saiyadian,M.S., Human Resources Management, New Delhi : Tata McGraw Hill,1988.

16. Austin (1987), Comparison of faculty perceptions of the workplace at low and high morale colleges: In A. P. Splete, A. E. Austin, and R. E. Rice (eds.), Community, Commitment and Congruence: A Different Kind of Excellence, The Council of Independent Colleges: Washington D.C.

17. Ansari, Baumgartel, and Sullivan (1982), "The personal orientation, organizational climate fit and managerial success", Human Relations, 35(12), pp.1159-1178.

18.　Likert (1961), New Patterns of Management, New York: McGraw Hill.

19.Thomas Moran and Fredricks Volkwein, J (1988), Examining Organizational Climate in Institutes of Higher Education, Research in Higher Education, Springer.

20. Ruth M. Guzley (1992), "Organizational Climate and Communication Climate Predictors of Commitment to the Organization", Management Communication Quarterly, May, vol. 5, no. 4, pp.379-402.

21. Cheryl L. Maranto, Andrea E.C. Griffin (1993), "The antecedents of a „chilly climate" for women faculty in higher education", Human Relations, February.

22. Agrawal, N.M. (1993), "Developing Work Cultures for High Involvement, High Performance Work Organizations", Vikalp, April.

23.Vijaya and Srinivasan (1996), "The relationship of Psychological Climate with Job Satisfaction and Organizational Commitment", Indian Journal of Applied Psychology, Vol.13.

24. Venkateswaran and Anantaraman (1996), "Organizational Climate and Industrial Accidents", Indian Journal of Applied Psychology, Vol.33, No.1.

25. Biswas, S.N. (1998), "Factors Affecting Training Effort: Influence of involvement, Credibility, Utility and Training, Transfer, Climate", Indian Journal of Training and Development, Vol.XXVII, No.4.

26.Mark A. Shadur, Rene Kienzle, John J. Rodwell (1999),"The Relationship between Organizational Climate and Employee Perceptions of Involvement", Group Organization Management, December, vol. 24, no. 4, pp.479-503.

27.Hoy, W. K., & Miskel, C. G. (2001), Educational administration: Theory, research & practice (6th ed.), New York: McGraw-Hill.

28. Abinash Panda and R.K. Gupta (2002), "Studying Organizational Culture: HICOM India", IIMB Management Review ,December, 14(4).

29.Agarwal, M., Bose, Sudeepa (2004), "Organizational climate for perceptions of procedural 'fairness' in human resource practices and role efficacy", Indian Journal of Industrial Relations, October, No.3.

30.Kirk L. Rogg, David B. Schmidt, Carla Shull and Neal Schmitt (2005), "Human resource practices, organizational climate, and customer satisfaction", Journal of Management, August, 31, pp. 492-512. 31.Andrew Neal, Michael A. West and Malcolm G. Patterson (2005), "Do Organizational Climate and Competitive Strategy Moderate the Relationship Between Human Resource Management and Productivity?" Journal of Management, August, 31, no. 4, pp.492-512.

32. McDuffie, J.P. (1995),"Human resource bundles and manufacturing performance: organizational logic and flexible production systems in the world auto industry", Industrial and Labour Relation Review, 48, pp. 197-221.

33. Wynn and Carboui (2006), Principal Leadership, school climate critical to retaining beginning teachers, Paper presented at the American Educational Research Association Annual Meeting, San Francisco.

34. Schulte, M., Ostroff, C., and Kinicki, A. J. (2006), "Organizational climate systems and psychological climate perceptions: A cross-level study of climate-satisfaction relationships", Journal of Occupational and Organizational Psychology, Volume 79, Issue 4, pp.645–671.

35. Richard E. Stup (2006), Penn State Dairy Alliance, Pennsylvania: The Pennsylvania State University.

36. Schulte, M., Ostroff, C., and Kinicki, A. J. (2006) op. cit. pp. 645–671.

37. Avinash Kumar Srivastav (2007), "Achievement Climate in Public Sector – A Cross functional Study on Relationship with Stress and Coping", IIMB Management Review, Volume 19, No. 4.

38. Graeme Currie and Andy Lockett (2007), "A critique of transformational leadership: Moral, professional and contingent dimensions of leadership within public services organizations", Human Relations, February, vol. 60, no. 2, pp.341-370.

39. King, E. B., De Chermont, K., West, M., Dawson, J. F., and Hebl, M. R. (2007), "How innovation can alleviate negative consequences of demanding work contexts: The influence of climate for innovation on organizational outcomes", Journal of Occupational and Organizational Psychology, 80(4), pp. 631–645.

40.Hui, C. H., Chiu, W. C. K., Yu, P. L. H., Cheng, K., and Tse, H. H. M. (2007), "The effects of service climate and the effective leadership behaviour of supervisors on frontline employee service quality: A multi-level analysis", Journal of Occupational and Organizational Psychology, 80(1), pp. 151–172.

41.Gonzalez-Roma, V., Fortes-Ferreira, L. and Peiro, J. M. (2009), "Team climate, climate strength and team performance. A longitudinal study", Journal of Occupational and Organizational Psychology, 82(3), pp. 511–536.

42. Judith S. McCormick, Sharon K. Parker (2010), "A multiple climates approach to understanding business unit effectiveness", Human Relations, 63(11), pp. 1771-1806.

43. Alison M. Konrad ,Kathleen Cannings ,Caren B. Goldberg (2010), "Asymmetrical demography effects on psychological climate for gender diversity: Differential effects of leader gender and work unit gender composition among Swedish doctors", Human Relations, 63(11), pp. 1661-1685.

44. Michael D. Thompson (2009), "Organizational Climate Perception and Job Element Satisfaction: A Multi-frame Application in a Higher Education Setting", Research in Higher Education, 41, pp. 95-116.

45. Soumendu Biswas (2010), "Commitment as a Mediator between Psychological Climate & Citizenship Behaviour", Industrial and Labour Relation Review, Vol. 45, No. 3.

46. Halpin and Croft, D. (1963), The Organizational Climate of Schools, Chicago: University of Chicago Press.

47. Hoppock, R. (1935), Job Satisfaction, New York.

48. Centers, R. (1948), "Motivational Aspects of Occupational Stratification", Journal of Social Psychology, 28, pp. 187-217.

49. Walker and Guest (1952), The men on the Assembly Line, Cambridge: Harvard University Press.

50. Trow (1957), "Autonomy and Job Satisfaction in Task Oriented Groups", Journal of Abnormal Social Psychology, vol.54, pp.204-209.

51. Sanford (1950), Authoritarianism and Leadership, Philadelphia: Institute of Research in Human Relations Publications.

52. Fred Luthans (1981), Organizational Behaviour, New Delhi: McGraw Hill Company Ltd.

53. Herzberg, F. (1957), Work and the Nature of Work, Cleveland: World Publishing.

54. Porter, L. W. (1961), "A Study of Perceived Need Satisfaction in Bottom and Middle Management Jobs", Journal of Applied Psychology, 45, pp. 1-10.

55. Guha, J.N. (1965), "Job Satisfaction among Shoe Factory Workers", Productivity, Vol.6, pp.64-89.

56. Palmore, E. (1969), "Predicting Longivity, A Follow-up for Age", Gerontology, Winter.

57. Perrow, C. (1970), Organizational Analysis: A Sociological View, Belmont: Wadsworth.

58. Armstrong, T. B. (1971), "Job Content and Job Content Factors Related to Satisfaction for Different Occupational Levels", Journal of Applied Psychology, 55, pp. 57-65.

59. Starcevjch, M. M. (1972), "Job Factor Importance for Job: Satisfaction and Dissatisfaction across Different Occupational Levels", Journal of Applied Psychology, 56, pp.20-25.

60. Narain, L. (1973), Managerial Compensation and Motivation, New Delhi: Oxford & IBM, pp.30-40.

61. Singh, A. P., and Srivastava, A. K. (1975), "Occupational Level and Job Satisfaction", Journal of Psychological Researchers, 70(2), pp. 56-59.

62. Mirza S. Saiyadain (1977), "Organizational Levels and Job Satisfaction", Vikalpa, Vol. 2, No.1, January, pp. 29-39.

63. Baldev R. Sharma (1980), "Determinants of Job Satisfaction among Industrial Workers", Vikalpa, Vol. 5. No. 1, January, pp. 16-19.

64. Sharma, R.D., & Jeevan Jyoti (2006), "Job Satisfaction among School Teachers", IIMB Management Review ,December, Volume 18, Number 4.

65. Fred Luthans (1981), Organizational Behaviour, New Delhi: McGraw Hill Company Ltd.

66. Solomon E (1996), "Private and Public Sector Managers: An Empirical investigation of Job Characteristics and Organizational Climate", Journal of Applied Psychology, Vol.1, pp.247-259.

67. Sharon K. Parker (2007), "That is my job" How employees' role orientation affects their job performance", Human Relations, March, 60(3), pp. 403-434.

68. Padmaja Palekar (2007), "Strategic Human Resource Management– An Indian Perspective", Review, Volume 19, Number 3.

69. Celio A. A. Sousa ,Willem F. de Nijs ,Paul H.J. Hendriks(2010), "Secrets of the beehive: Performance management in university research organizations", Human Relations, September , 63(9), pp.1439-1460.

70. Sushmita Srivastava (2011), "A Study of the Impact of Types of Job change On Perceived Performance of newly Rotated Managers: The Mediating Role of Job Change Dimensions", Management and Labour Studies, February, Vol.36, No.1,pp.73-98.

71. Venkat Rao, Gudivada and Devaki Devi,P. (2012), "Performance and Satisfaction: A Critical Analysis",Acta Universitatis Danubius Economica,2 (8),pp.5-13.

72. Christina R., and Dr.A.Umesh Samuel Jebuseelam (2012), "HRD: A key to organizational Effectiveness",Personnel Today,April-June,Vol.XXXIII(1),pp. 35-41.

73. Meera Shankar and Omer Bin Sayeed (2012), "Role of Transformational leaders as change agents: Leveraging effects on Organizational Climate", Indian Journal of Industrial Relations, Vol.47 (3), January, p.470.

74. Ashish Sinha and Bindu Arora (2012), "Fit between Organizational Culture and Business Excellence: A case Study of Heavy Electrical Equipment Plant, BHEL", Vikalpa, Vol.37 (3), July-September 2012, pp. 19-27.

75. Davar, S.C., and Ranji Bala (2012), "Relationship between satisfaction and performance: A meta-analysis", Indian Journal of Industrial Relations, Vol., 48(2), October, p.290.

76. Boh, Wai Fong and Wong, Sze Sze (2013), "Organizational Climate and Perceived Manager Effectiveness: Influencing Perceived Usefulness of Knowledge Sharing Mechanisms," Journal of the Associatiofor   Information   Systems,Vol.14(3),2.

77. Wang, J.L., Zhang, D.J. and Jackson, L. A. (2013), Influence of self-esteem, locus of control, and organizational climate on psychological empowerment in a sample of Chinese teachers, Journal of Applied Social Psychology, doi: 10.1111/jasp.12099.

78. Arun Kumar, P. (2002), Unpublished thesis submitted to Department of HRM, Andhra University.

79. Chan Kim W., and Renee M. (2009),"How Strategy Shapes the Structure", Harvard Business Review South Asia, September, p.60.

80. Udai Pareek (2007), Understanding Organizational Behaviour, New Delhi: Oxford University Press.

81. Baldev Sharma (1986), Not by Bread Alone, New Delhi, pp.26- 27.

82. Delaney & Huselid(1996), "The impact of human resource management practices on perceptions of performance in for-profit and nonprofit organizations", Academy of Management Journal, 39, pp. 949-969.

83.Perrow, C. (1970), Organizational Analysis: A Sociological View, Belmont: Wadsworth.

Chapter 3

Methodology

FRAMEWORK OF THE STUDY:

The present study is done to answer some of the problems mentioned in the research agenda. Climate is also concerned with the process, style of an organizational life, its content and substance. The above review of literature clearly points out that some more studies are required to understand organizational climate and its impact on perceived performance and job satisfaction. The organizational climate is an evergreen subject and changes with time. Further, studies on organizational climate and its impact on perceived performance and job satisfaction in a restructured organization in Indian context are incomplete. Therefore, organizational climate in a restructured organization at the unit level is taken up for the study.

The Indian business environment is passing through transition due to growth in world trade and integration of the world market. The shipbuilding industry in India is facing competition. The Hindustan Shipyard Limited is a premier shipbuilding organization on the east coast of India at Visakhapatnam. The Hindustan Shipyard Limited is a public sector organization and second largest shipbuilding yard in India. The government policy of liberalization has affected this organization financially due to decrease in order book.

The government in order to make it viable has announced restructuring package in 2008. As a part of restructuring package;

1. The firm was provided with financial assistance in 2010-11 and

2. The firm is transferred by the Government of India from the administrative control of Ministry of Surface Transport to Ministry of Defense in 2010.

The principle objective of the Ministry of Surface Transport is commercial production whereas that of Ministry of Defense is production for defense requirements. The environment of organizational change is to be tested and for this purpose, organizational climate and its manifestation with respect to Human Resource practices are chosen for the study. Since there is a change due to restructuring and transfer, Hindustan Shipyard Limited is selected as a sample for the study.

The human resources practices and the concepts were re-conceptualized for the present study as follows.

ORGANIZATIONAL CLIMATE:

The Organizational Climate is the summation of perceptions of the individuals. It is the reflection of the individuals" perception on Objectivity and Rationality,

Compensation, Grievance Handling, Working Conditions, Performance Management, Training and Development, Communications, Welfare, Relations and Job Design.

Objectivity and Rationality:

The objectivity in the policies, objectives and practices of human resources management and rationality in the choice of such policies, objectives and practices. The Objectivity and Rationality acts as a support climate and helps in perception of the employees towards positive or negative climate.

Compensation:

The compensation is the need satisfier or dissatisfies the employees. The compensation may be in cash or kind, variable or fixed. It is the pay or remuneration for the work done by the employee. The compensation is to be matched with the work done; otherwise it results in positive or negative climate.

Grievance Handling:

The grievance may arise due to variety of reasons either work related or not. Grievance may be substantial, real or imaginary. The grievances have negative fallout on the industrial relations, if not stitched in time. Grievance has to be handled properly to avoid dissatisfaction, industrial strife or conflict.

Working Conditions:

The working conditions relate to the health, safety and welfare facilities provided to the employee at work. The working conditions are statutory requirements; organizations provide extra facilities at work to motivate them for performance. The working conditions either satisfy or dissatisfy the employee at work and it manifests in positive or negative climate.

Performance Management:

The performance of an employee at work is to be evaluated, the performance has to be fixed, measured and evaluated. The management of performance also involves evaluating the performance and fixing rewards for performance.

Training and Development:

Training is the process by means of which aptitudes, skills and capabilities of individual employees to perform specific jobs are increased (T.N Bhogoliwala, 1990)[1] whereas development is concerned as the means by which a person cultivates those skills whose application will improve the efficiency and effectiveness with which the anticipated results of a particular organizational segment are achieved (Koontz H. and O. Donnel C., 1978)[2].

Communication:

The communication is the process by which the sender sends a message to the receiver. The vertical and horizontal flow of messages is the communication. The communication is to be understood in the same sense as the sender. The communication may be formal or informal, but it impacts the environment as a process or means that conveys the management mind to the employee.

Welfare:

According to Hopkins R. R., (1990)[3] welfare is fundamentally an attitude of mind on the part of management influencing the method by which management activities are undertaken. The welfare may be statutory or voluntary measures to enhance the health, safety and mental conditions at the work. The welfare measures include medical facilities, educational facilities, recreation, housing, transport and any other such measures that are in extra to the wages.

Relations:

The relations refer to the harmonious or non-conflict environment between employer and employee and between employee and employee.

Job Design:

The work has to be designed to include challenge, feasibility and simplicity. The worker should derive satisfaction from the work. The strategic orientation to job design is to make it adjustable to knowledge worker. In the present strategic environment, design of the job is an important factor.

JOB SATISFACTION:

The satisfaction derived by the employee from the job is job satisfaction. The Job satisfaction is an important parameter of measurement for organizational health. The term job satisfaction is holistic and inclusive with job autonomy, variety in skill and knowledge. The manifestation of job satisfaction may be felt on the individual, organization and the society.

PERCEIVED PERFORMANCE:

The term perceived performance means the feeling of work experience. The perceived performance is the way one perceives his performance at work. The performance is considered as comprehensive and includes discipline, performance on the job, guidance and counseling for performance, individuality means accomplishing work without dependence and planning and execution of the job on time. Therefore, for the purpose of this study, the following factors were conceptualized.

Discipline:

The term discipline is conceptualized to mean the ability to adhere to the terms and conditions of service.

Job:

The group of tasks and positions together form a job. For accomplishing the tasks effectively knowledge about the job and autonomy is essential. Therefore, the Job comprises the skills, abilities and knowledge.

Guidance and Counseling:

The term guidance and counseling refers to the ability of the person to guide and make one to one conversation with the subordinates to overcome work related problems.

Individuality:

The work requires certain level of independence as well as dependence, the individuality refers to the ability to accomplish task with least dependence on others and dependability for work i.e. the work is interrelated with other work.

Planning and Execution:

Planning is a conceptual skill required to direct future course of action. Whereas, execution means the ability to perform the work according to the stated plan.

RESEARCH DESIGN:

Hypothesis:

The following hypothesis were framed for the purpose of the study

1. There exist a relationship between the organizational climate, job satisfaction and perceived performance with the profile factors.

2. There exist an intra and inter-factor linkage between organizational climate, perceived performance and job satisfaction.

3. The organizational climate is positive and it is related with outcome variables such as job satisfaction and perceived performance in a shipbuilding unit.

4. The age, length of service of the personnel in public sector shipbuilding is high.

Objectives of the Study:

The research is being conducted with the following objectives.

1. To study the diversity factors in the profile of the respondents in the manufacturing unit.

2. To identify the influencing factors of organizational climate and perceived performance.

3. To study the intra and inter relationship between organizational climates, perceived performance and job satisfaction.

4. To identify the linkage between the organizational climate, perceived performance and job satisfaction with the profile factors respectively.

5. To study the impact of organizational climate on perceived performance and job satisfaction in the shipbuilding unit.

Profile of the Study Area:

The study area is located in the vicinity of Visakhapatnam City of Visakhapatnam District in Andhra Pradesh, which is one of the emerging cities in India. The City extends upto Pendurthi in south-west, Yarada in the South, Bay of Bengal in the East, and Boyapalem limits in the North. The climate is warm, the warmest months being April-June and the coolest in the State. The rainy season sets in the form of South-West monsoons. The Visakhapatnam city ranks second among the industrialized cities of Andhra Pradesh.[4]

The Hindustan Shipyard Limited, a Public Sector Shipbuilding Unit in Visakhapatnam is chosen as the study area. It was transferred from Ministry of Surface Transport to Ministry of Defense in May, 2010. The transfer has been affected as a part of restructuring exercise.

Therefore, Hindustan Shipyard Limited forms the universe for the present study.

Sample Size:

The size of the universe is 2,143. A sample of 15 percent i.e. 321 was selected for the study and the sample was drawn randomly from the universe. But, only 300 questionnaires were duly filled and returned in proper order. The returned questionnaires were approximately equal to 13.99 per cent of the universe. The rate of return is 94.5 per cent, this was considered reasonable for a study of this magnitude. The sample is selected from the permanent employees list provided by the organization.

Sources of Data:

The data required for the study is sourced from i) Primary Source and ii) Secondary Source

Primary Source:

The primary data required for the study is sourced through a questionnaire. The questionnaire is structured and framed for the purpose of eliciting the perception of the sample respondents. The questionnaire is a standard multiple choice questionnaire, the answers are arranged in the typical standard Likert style format[5] with five choices.

Further, personal interviews and general interaction methods were adopted to collect the necessary data required for the study.

Questionnaire Construct:

The questionnaire is constructed according to the requirements of the study and after referring standard formats prepared by Sinha, J.B.P.(1980)[6],Sharma, B. (1986)[7] and Devaki Devi, P. (2002)[8]. The questionnaire is prepared to elicit perception of the respondents and it is categorized into 3 parts.

1. Organizational Climate:

The instruments has 33 items covering 10 factors

i) Objectivity and Rationality

ii) Compensation

iii) Grievance Handling

iv) Working Conditions

v) Performance Management

vi) Training and Development

vii) Communications

viii) Welfare

ix) Relations

x) Job Design

2. Perceived Performance:

The instrument has 5 factors with 12 items.

i) Job

ii) Guidance and Counseling

iii) Planning and Execution

iv) Individuality

v) Discipline

3. Job Satisfaction:

The instrument has one inclusive question on Job Satisfaction.

Secondary Source:

The Company manuals were consulted for rules, regulations and guidelines of the organization. The company Websites, Social Media Network and e-journals were searched extensively for contemporary literature. Further, printed Journals, Magazines, Books and research publications were referred to review the literature. The

Government of India‟s publications were used to quote at the appropriate stages. The university library and public libraries were also consulted for the relevant literature.

STATISTICAL ANALYSIS:

Statistical Tools:

The data collected is analyzed using statistical tools. In the first step the data is tabulated using one and two - way tables. Later, the data is tested for its reliability using Cronbach‟s alpha. The Mean, a measure of central tendency is applied to calculate the realistic value of the factor. The chi-square is used sparingly to find the association between profile factors. In the next stage, the data is tested using multivariate technique called multiple regression analysis to establish the cause and effect relation and vice-versa. In addition, descriptive statistics like percentages are used where ever required.[9]

Data Analysis:

The data is analyzed using standard statistical package SPSS version 15.0 as follows
In the first stage, percentages and chi-square test are applied to analyze the profile of the respondents.

Later, in the second stage Mean is used to analyze the factors of organizational climate, perceived performance and job satisfaction. In the descriptive analysis with Mean test, the grading of mean value was divided into four slabs for easy understanding.

    1. >= 4 - High

    2. >= 3 - Moderate

    3. >= 2 - Average

4. < 2 - Low

In the third stage, multiple regression analysis is done with intra organizational climate variables, intra perceived performance variables, job satisfaction and profile variables.

In the final stage, multi regression analysis is applied to study the inter-relationship between organizational climate, perceived performance and job satisfaction.

Limitations of the study:

The research was conducted with the following limitations.

1. The request for confidentiality of information by the participants.

2. The inhibition of the employees to participate in the study.

3. The element of subjectivity involved in the scope of the study.

4. The employees are made to fill the questionnaire during working hours and consequently there were not able spend much time.

5. Some problems were encountered in finding the respondents selected through random sampling. The scope is limited to assess the perception of the employees towards the organization climate.

REFERENCES:

1.Bhagoliwala, T.N. (1990), Personnel Management and Industrial Relations, Agra: Sahitya Bhawan, pp. 293-295.

2. Koontz H., and O Donnel, C. (1978), Essentials of Management, Tata McGraw Hill: New Delhi, pp.350-351.

3. Hopkins R. R. (1990), as quoted by Sarma, A.M., in Aspects of Labor Welfare and Social Security, New Delhi: Himalayan Publications, pp.18-25.

4. Government of Andhra Pradesh, "A Handbook on Visakhapatnam District", Department of Information and Broadcasting, Andhra Pradesh, 2004.

5. Likert (1961), op.cit, pp.181-182.

6. Sinha, J.B.P. (1990), Work Culture in the Indian Context, New Delhi: Sage.

7. Baldev Sharma (1986), op.cit. pp.160 - 178.

8.Devaki Devi, P.(2002), Unpublished major research project,"Behaviour Dimension of Women at Work", Sponsored by University Grants Commission, Department of HRM, Andhra University.

9. Kothari, C.R. (1997), Research Methodology Methods and Techniques, Wishwa Prakashan: New Delhi, pp.104-105.

Chapter 4

Industry Profile

Organization Profile

INDUSTRY PROFILE:

In India, Shipbuilding Industry is traditional and has been flourishing for the last 6000 years; the earlier excavations found traces of shipbuilding at important places were Indus Civilization flourished. The British, Dutch and Portuguese"s rule over parts of Indian Territory saw the booming of this Industry. The ancient and medieval period literature on history mention the naval exploitation of the ruling Kings and the trade links with external world. The Andhra"s and the other south Indian kingdom"s Pandyan"s, Chola"s etc., indulged in naval expeditions and trade. This suggests that the shipbuilding flourished in those days.

The foreign travelers Marco Polo in 13th century and Nicole Conte in 15th century spoke of ships and the carrying capacities in their travelogue. In India, the first organized shipbuilding was established by a Parisee family of Lowjee Nassariee Wadia at Bombay and the activity flourished for a very long time. It acquired world renowned status and the yard built over more than 350 different types of ships. The Ships and Vessels may be categorized into Containers, Bulk Vessels, General Cargo Vessels, Tankers, Defense Vessels, Passenger Carriers and Oil Platforms. The Shipbuilding is a labor intensive sector.

The World shipbuilding Industry grew at the rate of 6 per cent between 1980 and 2005. The global order book for shipbuilding at the end of 2007 is 457 million DWT (Dead Weight Tonnage) with an average delivery of 60 million DWT. The shipbuilding industry has moved from the traditional shipbuilding countries to Korea, Japan and China. These emerging countries account for 85 per cent of deliveries. The world order book in 2009 shows, China (3523) has the largest bookings followed by

South Korea(1675) , Japan(1286), Europe (447),Vietnam(287) and India (287). India accounts for 1.36 per cent of gross tonnage and it is in the sixth position. The comparative productivity (dead weight tonnage per person) of Korea (320) is more than Japan (290), China (56) and India (50).[1]

In India, according to 2011 report more than Rs. 200 billion was committed for investment in shipyard yards by private and public sector companies.[2] During the period 1997-2002 the Indian shipbuilding Industry recorded a turnover of Rs.10,170 crores and the same has increased to Rs.36,570 crores for the period 2002-2007.[3] In India, there are thirty two shipyards out of which, six are under Central Government , two are under State Government, three are under public listed private shipyards and twenty two are privately held shipyards. Further, in the above units there are 20 dry docks and 40 slipways accounting for 2, 81,200 DWT capacity.[4]

In India, as on 1st September, 2012 there are four Defense shipyards namely Garden Reach Shipbuilders and Engineers Limited, Kolkata, Goa Shipyard, Goa, Mazagaon Dock Limited, Mumbai and the latest entrant Hindustan Shipyard Limited, Visakhapatnam.

The Cochin Shipyard Limited and the Hindustan Shipyard Limited has a capacity of 1.1 lakh DWT and 80,000 DWT respectively. In India, there are 35 registered ships repair units of which 7 are classified as major units.[5] The Hindustan Shipyard Limited is classified as major ship repairing unit.

GOVERNMENT POLICY ON SHIPBUILDING INDUSTRY IN INDIA

- The ship building subsidy scheme applicable to Indian Shipyards has expired and the Government of India has not renewed the scheme post liberalization.

- Further, the Government of India has discontinued the policy of awarding shipping orders on nomination basis to public sector units.

- The private sector is allowed into shipbuilding industry, Government support to the industry is concentrated on providing infrastructure.

- Foreign Direct Investment to the extent of 100 per cent is allowed in India.

ORGANISATION PROFILE:

BRIEF HISTORY:

Hindustan Shipyard Limited is strategically located in the east coast of India at Visakhapatnam, in Andhra Pradesh. The Shipyard was founded by Walchand Heerachand of Scindia Steam Navigation Company Limited; he along with Navrotem Moraji prepared a plan with the expert advice of Mr. Knudsen of England in 1921. However, the plan did not materialize and again in 1940, Shri Walchand Heerachand approached the then Government with the plan and due to the then prevailing conditions the Government accepted his proposal for establishing the shipyard at Visakhapatnam. The Shipyard at Visakhapatnam was started initially within an area of 56 acres and Messer"s Alexander Gibbs & Partners of Britain were the consultants.

The foundation stone was laid by Dr.Rajendra Prasad, the then President of Indian National Congress on 21st June, 1941. The work was interrupted due to war and again commenced in 1942. The Shipyard was started with an initial capacity of 16,000 DWT and has facilities for ship repairs and ship building. The first Prime Minister of independent India launched the first steam ship of 8,000 DWT capacity "S.S.JALA USHA" on 14th March, 1948. The shipyard faced financial difficulties and approached the Government for input subsidies, during the period 1948 to 1950. The shipyard has by then constructed 8 ships. Due to severe financial crunch Sri Shyama Prasad Mukherjee, Minister of Industry and Supply of Government of India announced the takeover of shipyard on 16th March, 1950. Thus, Messer"s Hindustan Shipyard

Limited came into existence on 21st January, 1952. The shares were owned by Government of India and the Scindia Steam Navigation Company Limited in the ratio of 3:1. Later, the company was nationalized and it became a wholly owned Government company in July, 1961.

After nationalization, the company embarked on an expansion plan by adding two more berths and additional facilities. The company engaged the services of French consultants, M/s Soeits Anenyme Des and M/s Atelieret Chantiera Dela Laire. Further, technical collaborations were made with LUBECKER FLANDER WEARKE to built LUBRNKENT class vessels up to 12,500 DWT. Later, modernization and expansion plans were initiated in 1969 and 1987. The construction capacity was increased to 50,000 DWT and a separate offshore platform building yard was built in the year 1985. In technical collaboration it got the knowhow to manufacture versatile class offshore platform from Norway based Messer"s Ulstein.

CHRONOLOGICAL ORDER OF DEVELOPMENT:

The important milestones achieved in the history of the company are as follows

1941 – Dr. Rajendra Prasad (the first President of India) the then president of Indian National Congress laid the foundation stone on 21/6/1941 for Scindia Shipyard at Visakhapatnam.

1942 – Keel Fork for the first steam ship "Jala Usha" was laid on 22/6/1946.

1947 –First steam ship of 8,000 DWT "Jala Usha" was launched by Sri Pandit Jawaharlal Nehru, the Prime Minister of India on 14/3/1948.

1952 – Major shares of Scindia Shipyard were taken over by Government of India and the firm is named as Hindustan Shipyard Limited.

1953 – Construction of diesel ships.

1958 – Completion of 1, 00,000 Gross Rated Tonnage with the delivery of M.V. "Jala Veela", the 23rd vessel.

1961 – HSL becomes fully owned Government of India enterprise in July 1961. 1972– Training ship "Rajendra" handed over to Smt. Indira Gandhi, the Prime

Minister of India.

1976 – Commission of West Basin adjacent to Dry Dock for float

repairs. 1979 – HSL paid dividend to government.

1979 – Commissioning of Hindustan Dry Dock for ship repairs (ships upto 70,000 DWT can be accommodated).

1983 – Laying of foundation stone for building dock on 28/8/1983 by Sri Vijaya Bhaskar Reddy, the then Minister for Shipping and Transport.

1985 – Inauguration of shore platform construction yard by Sri Gani Jail Singh, the President of India on 17/7/1985.

1985 - A highly sophisticated technologically complex drill ship, viz., Sagar Bhushan, for the Oil and Natural Gas Commission.

1986 – Flagging off of the first jacket built at Offshore Platform yard on 8/4/1986.

1987 – Inauguration of new covered building dock for construction of ships up to 50,000 DWT by Sri Gani Zail Singh, the President of India on 5/4/1987.

1988 – Flagging off the first Deck built at Offshore Platform yard on 3/1/1988. 1989 – Construction of the jacket in record time of 118 days.

1990 – Float out of the first vessel (a 42,750 DWT Bulker).

1993– Delivery of the 100th vessel M.V. "Lok Pratap" on 28/6/1993 at HSL Visakhapatnam.

1996– Delivery of M.V. "Maharashtra" (a 42,750 DWT Bulker) the largest vessel built by HSL on 6/1/1996.

1997– First shipbuilding yard in the country to be awarded the ISO-9001.

1998– Delivery of M.V. "Goa" (a 42,750 DWT Bulker) the largest vessel built by HSL on 15/1/1998.

1999– Delivery of M.V. "Swaraj Deep", 1,200 passenger cum-cargo vessel on 9/12/1999.

2000– Delivery of M.V. "Sardar Patel", T.B.T tug built by HSL on 27/5/2000.

2001– M.V. "Rangat", a passenger cum-cargo vessel delivered on 16/10/2001.

2002– M.V. "Baratang", a passenger cum cargo vessel delivered on 17/1/2002.

2003 –M.V. "Tiracol-II", a 45-T. B.P. Tug was delivered on 31/3/2003.

M.V. "Chouldari", delivered to Andaman & Nicobar Administration on 28/11/2003.

2004– M.V. "Teal", a passenger vessel was delivered on 24/2/2004.

First major repair of Jack up oil rig "Sagar Pragati" for ONGC.

2005– Modernization and medium refit of INS Sindhu Kirti, 877 EKM

Submarine.

2010- Deliver of 53,000 DWT Bulker to GML, Chennai

2010- Deliver of M.V. "Good Earth Pride" to GML, Chennai

2011- Deliver of M.V. "Good Earth Precedent" to GML, Chennai

2011- Mr.A.W.Delima, 50-T Bollard pull Tug to VPT, Visakhapatnam

2012- Deliver of M.V. "Good Trade" to GML, Chennai

Overhauling of giant oil rig worth Rs.500 crores for ONGC.

The shipyard has built 156 ships and repaired nearly 2000 ships.

RESTRUCTURING:

TRANSFER TO DEFENSE MINISTRY:

The Hindustan Shipyard Limited was transferred from the administrative control of Ministry of Shipping and Transport to Ministry of Defense in May, 2010. Henceforth, only Defense orders will be executed on completion of the existing orders.

FINANCIAL PACKAGE:

The Hindustan Shipyard Limited was given financial package of Rs. 824.90 crores, out of which Rs.452.68 crores was a grant to clear old loans and the remaining amount is categorized as loan in perpetuity.

VISION:

Before Restructuring:

To make HSL a World Class Shipyard with modernization and up gradation of infrastructure facilities.

After Restructuring:

2010-2011

To become a world class Defense Shipyard, to construct Naval Ships and submarines for the Indian Navy and Coast Guard and to meet the repair requirements of such vessels and other Government vessels.

Revised in 2011-12

To be a National Leader in Ship & Submarine building and Repairs.

MISSION:

Before Restructuring:

- To operate a strong and efficient shipbuilding, ship repairing and retrofitting of submarine to meet the growing requirements of mercantile, marine, Oil and Defense sectors with good management and improved efficiency.

- To attain core competency in 877 EKM submarine retrofit and modernization.

- To improve financial performance and profitability.

After Restructuring:

2010-2011

To upgrade the shipyard, acquire advanced technologies in war ships and submarine construction in a phased manner from 2010 to 2025, and take up projects planned by Indian Navy and Indian Coast Guard for meeting its long term needs.

Revised in 2011 – 12

To imbibe the latest in Ship / Submarine building and repair technology and serve the defense, maritime and oil sectors through all round excellence in quality, delivery and durability.

OBJECTIVES:

- To secure new ship building orders for naval ships and submarines.

- To undertake new construction and retrofitting of submarines.

- To prepare a modernization plan for construction of convential and strategic submarines.

- To augment technological capabilities in the area of ship design and ship construction.

- To train shipyard manpower on construction of Defense vessels.

- To incorporate "best practices" in all key activities of the yard including production, planning, purchase, marketing, human resources and customer satisfaction.

- To workout cost effective funding arrangements for shipbuilding and major ship repair projects.

- To implement e- procurement and e- payment.

- To effect economy in expenditure.

- To build up a strong ship building industry of the company with a view to contributing significantly to the growing requirement of national shipping.

- To develop among the employees consciousness of the environment, activate pollution control measures as necessary and monitor them.

- To ensure highest quality and international standard called for in ship building and ship repairs at competitive prices and prompt delivery.

MODERNISATION:

The modernization is to be taken up in two phases.

Phase – I:

- The existing infrastructures will be refurbished and obsolete equipments will be renewed.

- Construction of Landing Platform Dock for Indian Navy & Coast Guard.

Phase – II:

- Providing infrastructure to enable construction of sophisticated warships and strategic vessels.

THE INFRASTRUCTURE:

The ship yard has a carpet area of around 3, 00,000 square meters. The work flow is planned in such a way without any dysfunctions. The yard is equipped with the following machinery.

- The steel processing facilities consist of a stockyard to hold 30,000 tonnes of steel

- modern plate and section treatment plant

- gas cutting machines

- heavy duty presses

- self-evaluating trucks capable of handling blocks up to 250 tonnes

- large prefabrication shops with overhead traveling cranes of adequate capacity

- The hull construction facility includes a modern covered building dock and 3 shipways

- The long outfitting quay is equipped with attendant self-contained services and facilities i.e., hull outfitting, engineering and electrical ships

SHIPBUILDING FACILITIES:

The range varied from convention bulk carriers to general cargo and supply vessels, patrol vessels to highly sophisticated drill ship, covering Defense and oil sectors, apart from conventional merchant shipping tanks, highly sophisticated and complex drill ship. The construction of Landing Platform Dock was planned in the current year. The table 3.1 gives the details

Table 3.1

INFRASTRUCTURE FOR SHIPBUILDING

S.No	Facility	Size in Meters	Capacity (in tons DWT)
1	**Berth no.1**	195×26.6	30,000
2	**Berth no.2**	195×26.6	30,000
3	**Berth no.3**	140×22.7	Small crafts
4	**Covered building pack with intermediate gate facility**	240×53	80,000
5	**Outfitting quay**	460	2-3 ships up to 50,000 DWT

SHIP REPAIRS DIVISION:

The Ship Repairs division was commissioned in 1971 in technical assistance with Ishikawajma Harima Heavy Industries of Japan. The facilities are given in the table 3.2.

Table 3.2

INFRASTRUCTURE FOR SHIP REPAIRS

S.No	Facility	Length (In Meters)	Draft (In Meters)	Capacity (In tons DWT)
1	West Basin (South arm)	226	10	30,000
2	West Basin (North arm)	168	10	30,000
3	Outfitting quay	460	6	2-3 ships up to 50,000 DWT

SUBMARINE RETROFIT DIVISION:

The submarine retrofit was established in the year 1996; it caters to the needs of Indian Navy and is equipped to repair submarines.

OFF-SHORE PLATFORM DIVISION:

Hindustan Shipyard manufactures off shore oil and gas production platforms, it has advanced technologies and up-to-date facilities. In 1985, it has obtained technology from United Kingdom. Hindustan Shipyard can undertake offshore projects on turnkey basis covering design, procurement, fabrication, load out and installation.

All the above facilities are automated as per the requirements. The design section and production section is integrated with Computer Aided Design (CAD) and Computer Aided Manufacture (CAM) using AUTOKAN software. The ship design capability is augmented with workstations exclusively for piping, electrical and other outfitting requirement, which keep HSL on the forefront of automation in design and manufacture of ships. In technical collaboration with HSVA Ship Model Testing Establishment, Germany it built ships with "HS-Standard Flexible Design".

Hindustan Shipyard Limited has acquired capabilities to manufacture tankers, container vessels, dredgers, passenger vessels, survey vessels etc., up to 70,000 DWT.

QUALITY ASSURANCE:

The Hindustan Shipyard Limited was awarded ISO-9001 certificate by LLOYDS REGISTAR OF QUALITY ASSURANCE, London for construction of vessels up to 50,000 DWT and ISO-9002 for industrial structure in December, 1996. Further, the ships manufactured are certified as per the quality requirement of the customers.

REGISTERED AND CORPORATE OFFICE:

The registered office of Hindustan Shipyard Limited is located at 406, Vikram Tower, 16 Rajendra Palace, New Delhi-110 008 and the works are located at Gandhigram, Visakhapatnam. The Board of Directors is responsible for functioning of the organization. The Chairman cum Managing Director is responsible for running the day to day activities. The Chairman cum Managing Director and Board of Directors are appointed by Government of India with bureaucrats and Defense personnel.

THE BOARD DIRECTORS:

N.K. Mishra - Chairman cum Managing Director

Shri Rakesh Mahajan - Director (Finance and Commercial)

Cmde. K.S. Subramanian, NM, IN (Retd.)

- Director (Ship Building)

Cmde.K.L.N. Prasad, IN (Retd.)

 - Director (Corporate Planning & Personnel)

Cmde. Ashok Bhal, VSM, IN (Retd.)

 - Director (Strategic Projects)

Vice Admiral N.N. Kumar AVSM, VSM, IN

 - Director

Shri Gyanesh Kumar - Director

Dr. Devi Singh - Director

Company Sectary

FINANCIAL POSITION:

After restructuring, as on 31st March, 2012 authorized equity share capital is Rs. 304 crores and the subscribed share capital of the company is Rs.301.99 crores. The entire capital is subscribed by Government of India. The net worth of the company is negative (Rs. 714.00 crores). The company recorded a loss of Rs.85.98 crores on a turnover of Rs.604.34 crores in 2011-12.The wage and salary bill is Rs.3.41 crores and the amount spent on subsidized canteen is Rs.3.22 crores and on medical is Rs.7.10 crores. The employer provident fund contribution is Rs.5.2 crores. The accumulated losses as on 31st March, 2012 were Rs.1,016.08 crores.

In the year 2010 – 11, as a part of financial restructuring Rs.824.90 crores was paid by the Government of India, out of which Rs.452.68 crores was a grant to clear old loan and remaining is a loan in perpetuity. The company recorded a sales turnover of Rs.637.88 crores in 2010-11. The company reported a net profit of Rs.55 crores mainly due to Rs.314.31 crores grant provided by the Government of India as a part of restructuring. The accumulated losses as on 31st March, 2011 were Rs.930.10 crores.

Turnover:

The total turnover recorded in 2010-11 and 2011-12 is as given below.

Table 3.3

SALES TURNOVER

(Rs. In Crores)

Description	2010 -11	2011 -12
Ship Building	247.85	262.29
Ship Repairs	286.62	204.03
Retrofit	91.18	115.86
Unaccounted	12.83	22.16
Total	637.88	604.34

CAPACITY UTILIZATION:

The capacity utilization in 2009-10, 2010-11 and 2011-12 is 90 percent, 82 percent and 75 percent respectively. The actual production in 2011-12 is 56,437 DWT. The capacity utilization position is shown in the table 3.4. However, the productivity measured as man hours per dead weight tonnage has improved from 27.20 to 45.[6]

Table 3.4

CAPACITY UTILISATION

Capacity	2011-12	2010-11	2009-10
Installed Capacity (3.5 standard Pioneer Ships per Annum)	75,250 DWT	75,250 DWT	75,250 DWT
Actual Production	56,437 DWT	61,853 DWT	67,572 DWT
Capacity Utilization(Per Cent)	75%	82%	90%
Productivity(Man hours/DWT)	45	42.5	27.20

ORDER BOOK POSITION:

As on 31st March, 2012, the Hindustan Shipyard Limited has orders worth Rs.1,133.22 crores for 23 vessels. Further, Indian Navy placed orders worth Rs.4,000 crores for Landing Platform Vessels to be delivered by 2016.

ORGANIZATION STRUCTURE:

The Organizational Structure allocates authority, responsibility and its main objective in Hindustan Shipyard is for better utilization of resources. The organizational structure is both functional and production type. The Chairman cum Managing Director is assisted by General Manager, Deputy General Manager and others. The organizational hierarchy is tall and horizontal. The Hindustan Shipyard has job oriented layout and there unit manufacturing is done. And at material preparation stage cellular layout is followed.

The organizational structure is traditional and long. The firm is registered as company and it is under the overall control of Ministry of Defense, Central Government.

The Organizational Chart is provided in the following page.

DEPARTMENTS:

The activities in Hindustan Shipyard Limited is divided into 42 departments, the main departments are

FINANCE:

The finance department is entrusted with financial duties. It is divided into Pay Section, Wage and Salary Section, Provident Fund Section, Cash Section, Bills Section and Cost Accounts Section. The Internal and Pre-Audit section checks the financial transactions and liaisons with statutory authorities.

MARKETING:

In Hindustan Shipyard Limited, the orders are placed on competitive bidding and nomination basis. But, after it was transferred to Defense, all the Navy requirements are placed with Hindustan Shipyard Limited.

PRODUCTION:

The production department is divided into three sections.

> 1) **Steel Complex:** This section includes a)Hull Shop b) Prefabrication c) Erection d) Ship Wright e) Welding Skid Area, Berth and Jetty Area.

2) **Outfit Complex:** This section includes a) Hull Outfit consisting of Black-Smith section and Steel Outfit section b) Outfit Accommodation consists of sheet metal workshop and Painting c) Rigging.

3) **Engineering Complex:** This section has a) Electrical b) Plumbing c) Engineering.

PRODUCTION PLANNING AND PROJECT MANAGEMENT:

The activities in the department include planning of ship schedules, daily, weekly and yearly work progress report.

PURCHASE AND MATERIALS:

The purchase department will procure various materials for use in building of ships. Further, requirements for maintenance of plant and buildings are procured. The materials section will procure and store the material and issues materials based on indent. The material logistics are taken care by this department.

PERSONNEL AND ADMINISTRATION:

This department is divided into a) Workman Cell b) Staff Cell and c) Executive Cell. The personnel division is headed by General Manager (Personnel and Administration). The Deputy General Manager (Personnel and Administration), Managers of Staff cell, Executive cell and Training Department , Manager (Medical), Deputy Managers of Executive cell, Staff cell, Workmen cell, TLM cell, Co-ordination & Legal cell and Section officers of various cells and departments and senior personnel officers assist the General Manager in discharging duties. The functions of this department includes recruitment, promotion, transfers, establishment matters, disciplinary actions, legal matters, contract labor, implementation of various labor laws, time-keeping and leave management section, industrial relations, welfare, medical, transport, uniforms, canteen, guest house and housing estate.

DRY DOCK AND SHIP REPAIRS:

The department functions are to oversee the repair of various commercial and war ships, tugs, dredgers and fishing trawlers.

PLANT MAINTENANCE:

The duties and functions of this department are to maintain equipment and general maintenance works.

CIVIL MAINTENANCE:

Providing water, sanitation and domestic carpentry works to all the yards and colony.

SUBMARINE RETROFIT:

This department is carved to take care of the needs of Indian Navy works and activities include retrofit of submarine.

FIRE SERVICE AND SECURITY:

The department is equipped with full-fledged firefighting equipment to take care of the needs of the organization. The security of organization is also taken

care by this department.

LEGAL DEPARTMENT:

The legal matters relating to establishment, contracts and employees are the important functions of this department.

CONTRACTS AND COMMERCIAL:

The contracts and commercial aspects, relations with the owners and fulfillment of contractual obligations are the functions of this department.

QUALITY CONTROL:

This department has full-fledged equipment to take quality control measures at all stages in the construction of ships, certification by the agencies and specifications of the material used in the construction.

MANPOWER POLICY:

Hindustan Shipyard Limited has over five decades of reputation as a leading shipbuilding yard in India backed by professionalism and multi-disciplinary capabilities. It possesses a wealth of professionally qualified, competent and experienced workforce geared for construction of the most sophisticated ocean going vessels and other maritime structures. The workforce is continuously trained to upgrade its skills and technical know-how.

The skill and experience levels are backed by relevant academic and professional qualifications marked by versatility and rich experience in the various technical trades inherent to the ship building industry.

The specific objectives of manpower policy in the organization are

a) To achieve an effective utilization of human resources in the light of the organization goals.

b) To establish, maintain and review an appropriate organizational structure and develop desirable and productive working relationship among the members of the organization.

c) To ensure integration of the individuals into effective groups within the organization, by matching individual goals with those of the organization in such a manner that the employees feel a sense of involvement, commitment and loyalty towards it.

d) To generate maximum individual/ group development, within the organization by offering opportunities for advancement to employees through training, job rotation and career planning etc.

e) To recognize and develop approaches to satisfy individual aspirations and group expectations, providing scope for advancement commensurate with contributions, economic and social security, protection against hazards of life such as illness, old age, disability, death etc.

f) To maintain high morale and harmonious relations within the organizations by creating a suitable culture and improving the conditions of working.

GRADES AND DESIGNATIONS:

BOARD LEVEL OFFICERS:

Chairman cum Managing Director

Directors

SENIOR LEVEL OFFICERS:

Designation with Grade

Chief Vigilance Officer, Executive Director E8

General Managers E7

Deputy General Managers E6

Chief Manager E5

Managers E4

MIDDLE LEVEL OFFICERS:

Designation with Grade

Deputy Managers E3

Senior Engineers E2

Senior Engineers on Contract Basis

JUNIOR LEVEL OFFICERS:

Designation with Grade

Engineers E1

Engineers on Contract Basis

Section Officer E0

Management Trainee"s MT

STAFF:

Designation with Grade

Supervisory Staff -Technical

Supervisor, Assistant Supervisor,

Senior Draftsman, Quality Control Supervisor

Supervisory Staff –Non-Technical

Security, Fire and Sanitary Inspectors

Supervisory Staff - Technical (On Contract Basis)

Supervisor, Assistant Supervisor

Other Technical Staff

Switch Board, Sub-station, Dock Arm, Power House, Generator,

Plant Operators, Senior Lab. Assistants

Technical Trainees

Assistant Supervisor Trainees, Junior Draftsman Trainees

Clerical Staff - Non-Technical

Senior Assistant, Assistant, Junior Assistant

Casual Staff

Junior Assistant

Other Non-Technical Staff

Stenos, Typists, Medical Staff

Other Non – Technical Staff (On Contract Basis)

Para-Medical

WORKMEN:

Designation with Grade

Highly Skilled Workmen MTM, Senior MTM

Skilled Workmen TM –I, TM –II

Semi-Skilled Workmen Mates

Unskilled Workmen

Workmen (On Contract Basis) L or M Series

Workmen Working in Staff Cadre MDS

MANPOWER POSITION:

Grade with Number of employees

BOARD LEVEL OFFICERS:

Chairman cum Managing Director - 1

Directors – 7

SENIOR LEVEL OFFICERS:

E8 - 2

E7 - 6

E6 - 7

E5 - 21

E4 - 46

MIDDLE LEVEL OFFICER:

E3 - 62

E2 - 54

On Contract Basis - 11

JUNIOR LEVEL OFFICER:

E1 - 197

On Contract Basis - 29

E0 - 24

MT - 15

STAFF:

Supervisory Staff –Technical - 483

Supervisory Staff –Non-Technical - 25

Supervisory Staff – Technical - 27 (On Contract Basis)

Other Technical Staff - 60

Technical Trainees - 15

Clerical Staff - Non Technical - 121

Casual Staff - 1

Other Non – Technical Staff - 174

Other Non – Technical Staff - 6 (On Contract Basis)

WORKMEN:

Highly Skilled Workmen - 860

Skilled Workmen - 336

Semi-Skilled Workmen - 3

Unskilled Workmen - nil

Workmen (On Contract Basis) L or M Series - 563

Workmen Working in Staff Cadre - 51

Consolidated Strength of Manpower as on 01-04-2013

Officers Category

Regular - 375

Contract - 32

Total   - 407

Staff

Regular - 743

Contract - 31

Total   - 743

Workmen

Regular   - 1025

Contract -   651

Total   - 1676

Total

Regular - 2143

Contract - 714

Total - 2857

HUMAN RESOURCES MANAGEMENT IN HINDUSTAN SHIPYARD LIMITED:

PHILOSOPHY AND POLICY:

The Hindustan Shipyard Limited has an elaborate system in place to take care of human resource needs of the organization. The department plays a key role in formulating, implementing and evaluation of human resources policy in Hindustan Shipyard Limited. The policies cover wide ranging areas relating to human resource flow, reward system, work flow system and human development system.

The personnel and administration at functional level is headed by a Deputy General Manager and functions include personnel and industrial relations, administration and medical services. The functions are further grouped into a) executive cell b) staff cell c) workmen cell d) general and services and e) general administration.

HR DEPARTMENTS FUNCTIONS:

EXECUTIVE CELL:

The main functions of this cell are human resource planning, human resource procurement, placement, performance appraisal, confirmation, career planning, separations, discipline, wage and salary etc., and other matters of importance to the officers. The cell is headed by a manager, reporting directly to the Deputy General

Manager (Personnel and Administration) and assisted by deputy manager, section officer and 3 staff members.

STAFF CELL:

The main functions of this cell are human resource planning, human resource procurement, placement, performance appraisal, confirmation, career planning, separations, discipline, wage and salary of staff and also matters of establishment, all Government correspondence, statutory and non-statutory returns. The cell is also responsible for Time Keeping and Leave Management of Staff and Officers. The cell is headed by a manager, reporting directly to the Deputy General Manager (Personnel and Administration) and assisted by One Senior Personnel Officer, four assistants, one typist, stenographer and office attendant each.

WORKMEN CELL:

The workmen cell functions includes human resource planning, manpower procurement and development, performance appraisal, boundary management, separation settlement, disciplinary management, industrial relations, statutory requirements under industrial law and other matters of importance to the workers. This section is manned by Deputy Manager, one Section Officer, eight Senior Assistants and two office attendants.

CO-ORDINATION & LEGAL CELL:

The main functions of this cell are preparation, drafting of personnel policies, corresponding with the administrative ministries, legal cases pertaining to employees at various stages and voluntary retirement scheme.

HINDI CELL:

The main function of this cell is to implement official language i.e., Hindi as per the Central Government policy. This cell is headed by one Deputy Manager and assisted by One Senior Hindi Translator, One Assistant and One Senior Hindi typist.

TIME KEEPING & LEAVE MANAGEMENT CELL:

The workmen's attendance, late coming, absence and other leaves are under the administrative control of this cell. The cell operates under the administrative control of Deputy Manager and assisted by Senior Assistants and assistants.

WELFARE DEPARTMENT:

The department is being headed by Chief Welfare Officer in the organization. He is assisted by Two Senior Assistants and One Assistant in carrying out welfare activities. He will directly report to General Manager (P&A).The functions of grievance redressal are also carried out by Chief Welfare Officer with the assistance of One Senior Assistant.

The welfare department is responsible for complying with legal requirements.

MEDICAL REIMBURSEMENT SECTION:

This section is headed by Chief Welfare Officer. He is assisted by one Section Officer and five Senior Assistants and two Junior Assistants. This section looks after medical reimbursement facility to officers, staff and workmen of the organization.

SC/ST CELL:

The cell administers all matters relating to Schedule Castes and Schedule Tribes. It maintains all records pertaining to the above communities and complies with statutory requirements. The cell is also in charge of complying with the statutory requirements of Other Backward Castes and Physically Challenged. The cell is in overall administrative control of Manager (personnel) and is assisted by one Senior Assistant.

PERSONNEL CELL – DRY DOCK & SHIP REPAIRS:

This section deals with all personnel and administrative matters of employees in dry dock and ship repairs division.

TIME OFFICE MANAGEMENT:

HOURS OF WORK AND SHIFT TIMINGS:

There are two shifts and one general shift for all departments except the Service Department. The Service Department operates in three shifts. The shift timings are as stated below.

Production and Administration:

A Shift 7:00 am to 3:45 pm

B Shift 2:00 pm to 10:00 pm

General shift 8:00 am to 4:00 pm

Service Department:

A Shift: 6:00 am to 2:00 pm B

Shift: 2:00 pm to 10:00 pm C

Shift: 10:00 pm to 6:00 am

A lunch break of 45 minutes duration is provided. The shift rotation is effected in clock wise direction.

OVERTIME:

The employee will be allowed to do overtime for 2 hours a day as per contingencies of work.

LATE COMING:

Late coming is allowed up to 5 minutes, beyond that period deduction will be made at proportionate rate. Any employee who comes late for more than 5 times in a month will be referred to disciplinary committee.

LEAVES AND HOLIDAYS:

The employee can avail 3 types of leaves.

1. Earned Leave: The employees are eligible for 14 days earned leave in year depending on the number of days present. The earned leaves are calculated as per the Factories Act, 1948. Those who do not avail the leave are eligible for leave encashment at the end of the year and can be carried forward.

2. Casual Leave: The employee can avail 8 days casual leave in a calendar year.

3. Sick Leave: The employees are allowed to take 12 sick leaves and 24 half – day sick leaves. The half days may be commuted as 12 days.

HOLIDAYS:

The company shall declare 17 days as holidays, of which 14 days are festival holidays and 3 days are national holidays. These holidays are declared in consultation with the trade unions at the beginning of the year.

RECRUITMENT PROCESS:

The recruitment and selection is taken care by the executive cell, staff cell and workmen cell respectively in accordance with recruitments. The current policy is to recruit the right candidate at the right time and at the right place. The recruitment policy of the organization are following a) conformity with organizational objectives b)flexible systems c) matching work requirements with appropriate skills d) job analysis in right perspective and e) fairness in treatment to all employees' internal requirements and promotions.

SOURCING OF HUMAN RESOURCES:

The human resources can be sourced through Internal and External sources.

Internal sources:

The internal sources means the existing employees, the employee inventory is made as a part of forecasting. The inventory is made on skill availability, qualifications and demonstrated abilities. The employees with necessary competencies are sourced through internal recruitment.

External sources:

The external sources are chosen based on the type of job. The recruitment is done in Hindustan Shipyard Limited through two sources a) Advertisement in newspapers and employment news b) Employment Exchange as per the provisions of Employment Exchanges (Compulsory Notifications of Vacancies) Act, 1959.

SELECTION AND ISSUE OF APPOINTMENT ORDER:

The selection is based on the recommendations of the selection committee and it is purely merit based system. The appointing authority is Chief Manager (Personnel) for all the categories of workman and staff category. But, for executive cadre upto manager grade, Chairman and Managing Director is the competent authority to make appointments, from Chief Manager and above the Board of Directors will make the appointments.

INDUCTION PROGRAMME:

The Induction programme is conducted by the training department, the duration of the programme depends on the category and for new recruits the duration is one year. The main objectives of the training programme are 1) to socialize the new recruit to the organization culture and practices 2) to make the new recruit understand the working of different departments and 3) to impart conceptual, technical and behavioral skills.

The induction programme is divided into 3 modules M-I, M-II and M-III. The M-I module is for a duration of 1 month, M-II module is rotation training in different departments for 5 months and M-III training is on the job training for a duration of 6 months. The placement of the trained employee is based on the principle of right person for the right job and at the right place.

PERFORMANCE APPRAISAL:

The performance appraisal is done through annual confidential reports. The performance appraisal is done by the reviewing authority. The reporting/reviewing authority can review the confidential report of an employee, if he has at least an experience of 3 months of work.

TRAINING AND DEVELOPMENT:

The training center of Hindustan Shipyard Limited was established in the year 1956. The main objective of the training center is to train skilled technicians, tradesmen, marine engineers and other staff as per requirement.

The training department is under the control of General Manager (DDO & Training) and is well assisted by Manager (training), two section officers, six technical staff and two non-technical staff.

The Training Center is equipped with well built infrastructure viz., auditorium hall, conference hall and workshop to conduct programmes. The training schemes in Hindustan Shipyard Limited are as follows

1. STATUTORY TRAINING SCHEME:

Under this scheme, training is given in different trades like fitter, welder, electricians etc., the trainees are covered under Apprenticeship Act, 1961. The duration of the training period is one year. The trainees are paid a stipend at the rate of Rs.1, 240 per month for welders and Rs.1, 440 per month for fitters.

2. COMMERCIAL TRADE APPRENTICES:

Training in commercial trades like book keeping and accounting, store keeping (including purchasing) and clerical trades are provided to the commercial trade apprentices under the Apprentices Act, 1961.

3. ENGINEERING GRADUATES AND DIPLOMA APPRENTICES:

The training center also provides training to engineering and diploma holders and stipend is paid to the apprentices at rate of Rs. 1,850 per month for technical apprentices and Rs. 1,400 per month for apprentices on shipwright patterns.

Apart from the above, other different types of training programmes conducted at Hindustan Shipyard Limited are

1) Workers Awareness Programmes

2) Supervisory Development Programmes

3) Management Development Programmes

4) Marine Apprenticeship Training Scheme

5) Sandwich Apprentices Programme

6) All India Engine Cadet Training

7) Industrial Radiography Testing Safety Aspects

8) Welding Qualification Tests

9) Deputation for Training, Seminars, Conferences.

10) Advanced Vocational Training Programmes

11) Computer Awareness Programmes

All the above training programmes vary in period and they had to sign a bond.

PROMOTION POLICY:

The promotion policy is based on seniority cum merit. The main objectives of the promotion policy are

1) To provide broad opportunities for career growth and prospects of the employees.

2) To ensure fairness, consistency, uniformity and equitability in the matter of promotion of employees.

3) To recognize and reward employees by providing and maintain an appropriate environment for the effectiveness, efficiency and satisfaction of its employees, consistent with their contribution to the growth of the organization.

4) To create and sustain the morale of the employees by informing them of the kind of career promotion opportunities that exist in the organization and the basis of the manner in which such promotions will be effected.

The average of the rating from the annual confidential reports for the preceding 3 years will be taken into consideration for determining the qualifying levels. A score of 80 marks out of 120 in annual confidential report on average for three years are considered for promotion. The promotion from one grade to another will be subject to interview by the departmental promotion committee. The committee will evaluate the candidate for the remaining 20 marks. The employee has to obtain a total of 60 marks in interview and in annual confidential report to be eligible for promotion from one grade to another. In case of technical personnel, the candidates will undergo trade test or competency test and its assessment will be for 20 marks.

The entire yard is considered as one single unit for the purpose of determining the number of posts in each category for promotion within that cadre. The rules and eligibility norms for workman are

1) An unskilled worker who has drawn three increments in his grade will be eligible for test for promotion to semi-skilled category.

2) A worker who has drawn three increments in his grade will be eligible for test for promotion to tradesman II (skilled) category.

3) Tradesman II (skilled) for all trades (including skilled welders, gas cutters and technicians) who have put in seven years in tradesman II grade eligible for selection to tradesman I (selection grade asst. supervisors).

4) Promotions in all the above cases are subject to trade test and suitability of the candidate for promotion is determined in the manner laid in this procedure.

TRANSFERS:

In Hindustan Shipyard Limited, transfers are confined only to internal departments, the number of transfers made in 2010 and 2011 are 40 and 29 respectively. These transfers are need based transfers.

WORKING CONDITIONS:

As per the Factories Act, 1948, Hindustan Shipyard Limited is a factory. The health, safety and welfare measures as prescribed by the legislation are to be maintained in the organization.

HEALTH MEASURES:

In Hindustan Shipyard Limited, as per the Factories Act 1948, all the health measures are being implemented in the premises. The following health provisions are provided a) cleanliness b) ventilation c) lighting d) artificial humidification e) temperature f) no overcrowding g) latrines and bath rooms separately for males and females h) clean drinking water and i) spittoons.

SAFETY:

Safety policy of the organization:

The safety pledge is taken by all the employees. The safety guidelines are published in a form of booklet and supplied to all the employees. Further, regular safety and fire drills are conducted in the organization. The safety of all employees is one of the prime concerns of the company. Human life is invaluable and safety of human life and limbs is of overriding importance whatever may be the compulsion of business. In HSL, bilateral safety committees are constituted to suggest measures of safety at the work place. Every week, one safety awareness training programme is conducted for 30 members, safety messages are displayed on the board and walls. The national safety day is celebrated on 4th March every year and annual safety awards are given to the employees.

Safety Measures:

The Factories Act, 1948 has imposed obligation on the employer to implement certain safety measures at the work place. In Hindustan Shipyard Limited, the following safety measures are being implemented as required from section 21 to section 40. The below personal protective equipment are provided.

1. For head protection, safety helmet is provided.

2. For hand protection, hand gloves made of canvas leather.

3. For eye protection, heat protected glasses are provided.

4. For leg protection, industrial safety shoes and gumboots are provided.

5. For body protection, two pairs of boiler suits per year.

6. For nose protection, nose masks, respirations etc., to suit their working conditions.

EMPLOYEE WELFARE:

In Hindustan Shipyard Limited, welfare facilities are provided to the employees in the form of statutory welfare measures and non-statutory welfare measures.

STATUTORY WELFARE MEASURES:

The Factories Act, 1948 prescribes welfare measures or requirements under sections 42 to 49.

1) Washing facilities: The washing facilities are provided at the appropriate places as per the requirements in the yard and administration blocks.

2) Storing and drying facilities: The place for storing employees personal belongings are provided at the appropriate places.

3) Sitting facilities: The sitting facilities are provided at the appropriate points with makeshift shelters, where work is done in standing postures time breaks are given to take rest at the sitting shelters.

4) First-Aid box appliances: The first aid boxes with required material as per the relevant factory rules are maintained at the supervisor or foreman's office and at important work spots. A dispensary cum first aid centre with modern amenities with qualified medical officers and staff is provided for administering first aid.

5) Canteen: Two canteens with required amenities as per the Factory Act, 1948 are maintained inside the factory. The canteen is fully subsidized and meals, coffee, tea etc., are provided at reasonable rates.

6) Shelter, Rest rooms and Lunch rooms: As per requirement, lunch rooms are provided with adequate facilities separately for men and women. Further, separate facilities are provided for workmen, staff and officers.

7) Creches: This facility exists inside the premises, but for the time being it is not in working condition as they are no users for this facility.

8) Welfare officers: The Welfare Officers, Assistant Welfare Officers are appointed as per the requirements.

NON-STATUTORY WELFARE MEASURES:

The non-statutory welfare measures are provided by the organization according to its capacity. The non-statutory welfare measures are provided in Hindustan Shipyard Limited.

Housing facilities:

Hindustan Shipyard Limited has a full-fledged township at Scindia Colony; the quarters are grouped according to the rank of the employee separately for workmen, staff and officers. There are about 1900 quarters, two shopping complexes, and auditorium in the housing colony.

Educational Facilities:

The organization is managing educational institutes for the benefit of the children of the company; these educational institutes are managed on the advice of the bilateral committees. Further, educational allowance is provided for children's education.

Recreational Facilities:

Recreational facilities are provided to the employees. An auditorium and guest house is also provided in the colony.

Medical Facilities:

Hindustan Shipyard Limited is providing well equipped medical facilities. The medical facilities are free and consist of the following facilities.

1) Medical Hospital in the Housing Colony

2) Dispensary at the Yard

3) Referral Hospital and

4) Panel Doctors

The medical facilities are free for the employees and their wards. The medical hospital in the housing colony runs round the clock. The employees and their wards can avail outpatient treatment from the panel doctors. The medicines are supplied at the dispensary free of cost.

Occupational Health Service:

The occupational health service makes regular health check on the employees to find whether the employees are affected by any occupational diseases. The clinical check up is done once in a month in hazardous prone areas.

COMPENSATION:

The compensation for the employees consists of the following wage components.

1. Basic Pay

2. Dearness Allowance

3. House Rent Allowance

4. City Compensatory Allowance

5. Fitment Benefit

6. Other Allowances.

There are 50 different types of allowances paid to employees according to their grade, cadre and applicability.

The wage structure is as given below. The wage agreements are done at industry level for workers and staff. The executive wage structure is negotiated with executive body at the national level.

Board Level:

1. Chairman and Managing Director - Rs. 75,000 - Rs. 90,000

2. Director - Rs. 65,000 - Rs. 75,000

Executive Level	
Category	Wage scale
E0	Rs.12,600 - Rs.32,500
E1	Rs.16,400 - Rs.40,500
E2	Rs.20,500 - Rs.46,500
E3	Rs.24,900 - Rs.50,500
E4	Rs.29,100 - Rs.54,500
E5	Rs.32,900 - Rs.58,000
E6	Rs.36,600 - Rs.62,000
E7	Rs.43,200 - Rs.66,000
E8	Rs.51,300 - Rs.73,000

Staff Level	
Grade	Wage Scale (Rs.)
S1	4,200 - 75 - 6,600
S2	4,380 - 85 - 7,015
S3	4,670 - 95 - 7,420
S4	4,765 - 105 - 7,705
S5	4,970 - 115 - 8,075
S6	5,185 - 125 - 8,435
S7	5,400 - 140 - 8,760
S8	5,640 - 165 - 10,095
S9	5,890 - 175 - 10,440
S10	6,310 - 190 - 11,060
S11	6,450 - 195 - 11,325

Workmen Level	
Grade	Wage Scale (Rs.)
W1	4,200 - 75 - 6,600
W2	4,380 - 85 - 7,015
W3	4,765 - 105 - 7,705
W4	4,970 - 115 - 7,960
W5	5,490 - 125 - 8,490
W6	5,560 - 140 - 8,640
W7	5,710 - 165 - 9,670
W8	5,775 - 170 - 9,855

The dearness allowance is calculated on the basis of consumer price index for industrial workers, further deductions are allowed in accordance with Payment of Wages Act, 1936. The increments are made every year on 1st January or 1st July whichever is applicable. The stagnant increment is provided at the rate of 3 percent, limited to a maximum of three increments.

PROVIDENT FUND:

The employee and employer are contributing to provident fund at the rate of 12 percent each, and the accumulated amount along with interest is paid at the time of retirement. The provident fund is managed by a trust.

BONUS:

Attendance Bonus is paid to the staff and workmen who had not taken more than 5 leaves in a calendar year, leaves include all types of leaves. The employee is eligible for one day wage as attendance bonus. The employees are also eligible for bonus under the Payment of Bonus Act, 1965.

GRIEVANCE REDRESSAL PROCEDURE:

In Hindustan Shipyard Limited, grievance redressal cell is constituted as per the requirements. The grievance in Hindustan Shipyard Limited is tackled at 3 levels.

At the first level, a senior engineer or officer is designated as grievance officer, the grievance is submitted through written format or orally. The unsolved grievance is referred to Zonal level grievance committee which has to be redressed within 15 days of its receipt. The Chief Manager will be the committee head at Zonal Level. The third level is headed by the General Manager. The step ladder policy is followed in Hindustan Shipyard Limited.

INDUSTRIAL RELATIONS:

The Industrial Relations climate in Hindustan Shipyard Limited is cordial and harmonious. No strikes or lockouts were reported during the last 3 years. The Union is recognized through secret ballot, elections are held every three years. The collective bargaining process is given more importance and regular meetings are held.

In Hindustan Shipyard Limited, there are 13 registered trade unions and these are affiliated to different political parties. The Hindustan Shipyard Workers Union affiliated to Indian National Trade Union Congress is the recognized union. The major demands of the union like transfer to Defense ministry and new wage scales are recently implemented by the Government.

JOINT COMMITTEES:

The organization gives importance to Workers Participation in Management. The committees are bilateral with the representatives of management and workers. The workers representatives are nominated by the recognized union.

The following committees are in vogue in Hindustan Shipyard Limited.

1. Colony Improvement Committee

2. Safety Committee

3. Education Committee

4. Canteen committee

DISCIPLINE PROCEDURE:

In Hindustan Shipyard Limited discipline is given utmost importance, the standing orders is followed for defining the rules to be followed at the work place. The disciplinary procedure involves the following steps,

1. Framing of Charges

2. Domestic Enquiry procedure

3. Show Cause Notice

4. Disciplinary Action.

The enquiry officer after conducting the enquiry, reports to the disciplinary authority for action. The appeal against the disciplinary authority lies with the appellate authority.

QUALITY MANAGEMENT:

Quality Policy: To produce consistently to quality at national and international standards, and strive for customer satisfaction.

The quality objectives of the management are

1. Identify and Plan the relevant process for effective improvement of systems.

2. To meticulously plan the usage of resources in a competent and efficient manner.

3. Measure employee performance for continuous improvement.

4. Inspect, verify at different stages in the processes.

5. Internal audit in documented quality system procedure.

Quality certificate:

Hindustan Shipyard Limited has achieved the ISO-9001 quality accreditation certificate in construction awarded by Lloyds Register of Quality Assurance. The certification was renewed with regularity. The quality management system of ISO-9001:2000 standard is being maintained through periodical internal audits by quality internal auditors.

REFERENCES:

1. KPMG, Report on Indian Shipbuilding Industry: Poised for Take Off? Global Conference and Exposition on Shipbuilding, Submitted to FICCI, 2007, Mumbai.

2. Export Import Bank of India, Occasional Paper No.142, Indian Shipping Industry: A Catalyst for Growth, October, 2010.

3. ibid.., pp.10-15.

4. ibid.., pp. 20-21.

5. Government of India, Report of Working Group for Shipbuilding and Ship Repair Industry for the Eleventh Five Plans (2007 -2012), March, 2007.

6. Human Resource Manual, Hindustan Shipyard Limited.

7. 60th Annual Report, 2011-12, Hindustan Shipyard Limited.

8. 59th Annual Report, 2010-11, Hindustan Shipyard Limited.

Chapter 5

Analysis of Profile Factors

Data analysis is the process of subjecting the data to statistical calculation and interpretation. Data analysis means coding the data, tabulating the data, testing the data and interpreting the data. The data collected is to be tested for its reliability.

RELIABILITY TEST:

Therefore, the data is tested for its reliability using Cronbach"s Alpha reliability test.

The Cronbach Alpha score of above 0.60 is generally considered as reliable for the studies of this magnitude.

The reliability coefficients for socio-economic variables, organization climate variables, perceived performance variables and total variables in the shipbuilding unit are 0.678, 0.856, 0.811 and 0.757 respectively. The coefficients are within the acceptable limits for a study of this magnitude. The table 5.1 shows the details.

Since all the variables are within the acceptable limit the data relating to socio-economic variables, organizational climate, perceived performance and total variables are reliable. The study is presented in the following sections.

Table 5.1 Cronbach's Alpha

Firm	Reliability Coefficients							
	Socio-Economic Variables		Organizational Climate Variables		Perceived Performance Variables		Total Variables	
	No. Of Item	Alpha	No. of Items	Alpha	No. of Items	Alpha	No. of Items	Alpha
HSL	16	.6781	32	.8567	12	.8114	77	.7571

Further, the data is analyzed under the following heads for convenience and simplicity.

I.   **Profile Analysis**: The profile variables consist of socio-diversity data, economic data, demographic data and employment data. Further, for easy reference and presentation the data relating to Shipbuilding unit are presented with their factors and criteria. The profile is analyzed by using the following statistical tools i) frequency tables ii) percentages iii) cross tables and iv) Pearson"s chi-square test. The frequency tables are tabulated as per requirement using grouped and ungrouped method. Further, wherever required cross-tables are used for examining the relation between variables. As and when necessary the significance of association between the variables is found using the chi-square test.

II. **Organizational Climate Analysis:** The mean score of each factor and organizational climate is calculated. The intra- relationship between the factors of organizational climate is tested with multiple regression models. Further, the impact of profile factors on organizational climate is also analyzed.

III. **Perceived Performance Analysis:** The mean score of each factor and perceived performance is calculated. The intra-relationship between the factors of perceived performance is tested with multiple regression models. Further, the impact of profile factors on perceived performance is also analyzed.

IV. **Job Satisfaction Analysis:** The mean score of job satisfaction is calculated and the impact of profile factors on job satisfaction is analyzed.

V.**Organizational Climate, Perceived Performance and Job Satisfaction Inter-Relationship:** The inter-relationship between organizational climate, perceived performance and job satisfaction is examined by applying multiple regression analysis.

I.   PROFILE ANALYSIS: SOCIO-
DIVERSITY FACTORS:

Age- Gender: The age profile in the shipbuilding unit is concentrated in the age group 50 years and above. The mean age of the sample is 45.33 years. Further, the mean age of the male and female respondents is 41.02 years and 48.38 years respectively. The percentage of respondents in the age group 20-30, 30-40 and 40-50 years are 12 per cent, 18 per cent and 22.7 per cent respectively. A substantial number of respondents (47.3 per cent) are in 50 years and above age group. The table 5.2 shows the details.

The gender wise analysis is done to know the gender variation and diversity in the sample. In the unit, the gender male with a representation of 72.0 per cent is in majority compared to females (28.0 per cent).

The Gender - Age analysis of Shipbuilding unit reveals interesting facts on the diversity of the respondents, within 20- 30 years age group 88.9 per cent and 11.1 per cent are males and females respectively. The males are dominant in all the category groups and maximum in 20 – 30 age group (88.9 per cent). The maximum numbers of females (32.4 per cent) are in the age group 40 – 50 years and minimum (11.1 per cent) in the entry level group i.e. 20 – 30 years age group. Further, Pearsons Chi-square value between the two variables age and gender is 3.238 and is significant at 5 per cent level with P-Value 0.356. The table 5.2 gives the data on gender and age linkage.

Table 5.2 Gender - Age

Gender	Age in Years				Total
	20-30	**30-40**	**40-50**	**50 and above**	
Male	32	40	46	58	216
	88.9%	74.1%	67.6%	69.0%	72.0%
Female	4	14	22	44	84
	11.1%	25.9%	32.4%	31.0%	28.0%
Total	36	54	68	142	300
Per cent within Age	100.0%	100.0%	100.0%	100.0%	100.0%
Percentage within Total	12.0%	18.0%	22.7%	47.3%	100%

Pearsons Chi-Square: Value 3.238, Degrees of freedom 3, P-Value .356

Gender- Caste: In the unit within male, general category is dominant (40.7 per cent) followed by backward caste (37.0 per cent), schedule castes (14.8 per cent) and schedule tribes (7.4 per cent). Again within female category, majority belong to general category (45.2 per cent) followed by backward castes (31.0 per cent), schedule castes (16.7 per cent) and schedule tribes (7.1 per cent). The data is referred from table 5.3. The Pearsons Chi-Square association is significant at 5 per cent level with P - Value 0.912.

Nature of work- Gender: In the unit, the percentage of respondents with non-technical qualifications is more in females (57.1 per cent) than males (32.4 per cent). Further, the percentages of respondents with technical qualifications are male (67.6 per cent) and female (42.9 per cent).

Gender – Nativity: The gender data on nativity in shipbuilding unit is analyzed. The results show that about 47.2 per cent of males and 40.5 per cent of females belong to Visakhapatnam. The rest are not natives i.e., 52.8 per cent males" and 59.5 per cent females" are from outside and the same are inferred from table 5.4. So, on the whole 45.3 per cent originally belong to Visakhapatnam and the rest 54.7 per cent are non-natives.

Marital Status: In the shipbuilding unit as the mean age is high, majority of the respondents are married (87.3 per cent). In shipbuilding unit, 85.2 per cent of males and 92.9 per cent of females as a percentage within the gender group are married. The details are shown in table 5.5.

Table 5.3   Caste – Gender

Caste	Gender		Total
	Male	Female	
General	88	38	126
	40.7%	45.2%	42.0%
Backward Castes	80	26	106
	37.0%	31.0%	35.3%
Schedule Castes	32	14	46
	14.8%	16.7%	15.3%
Schedule Tribes	16	6	22
	7.4%	7.1%	7.3%
Total	216	84	300
	100.0%	100.0%	100.0%

Pearsons Chi-Square: Value 0.533, Degrees of freedom 3, P-Value .91

Table 5.4   Gender – Nativity

Nativity	Gender		Total
	Male	Female	
Visakhapatnam	101	34	136
	47.2%	40.5%	45.3%
Non-Visakhapatnam	114	50	164
	52.8%	59.5%	54.7%
	216	84	300
Total	100.0%	100.0%	100.0%

Table 5.5   Marital Status- Gender

Marital Status	Gender		Total
	Male	Female	
Married	184	78	262
	85.2%	92.9%	87.3%
Unmarried	32	6	38
	14.8%	7.1%	12.7%
Total	216	84	300
	100.0%	100.0%	100.0%

Religion-Caste Analysis: The religion wise distribution in the shipbuilding unit shows the religion Hindu in majority (89.3 per cent). The Christians and Muslims are 8.0 per cent and 2.7 per cent respectively. The belief, values and ethics of the human being is better understood by knowing the religious affinity. In the shipbuilding unit, within Hindus" 42.5 per cent, 36.6 per cent 14.2 per cent and 6.7 per cent belong to General, Backward Caste, Schedule Caste and Schedule Tribe respectively. Majority of the Christians are either schedule caste or schedule tribe. The Christians are spread over in all the castes. The Muslims are in general and backward caste only. The table 5.6 shows the details.

EDUCATIONAL FACTORS:

Education: In the shipbuilding unit, majority (56.0 per cent) of them has technical qualifications, 39.3 per cent of the respondents have non-technical qualifications and a minute size of 4.7 per cent have technical and non- technical qualifications. Among the respondents, post graduates, graduates, Intermediates, SSC/10th and Below SSC with General Educational Qualifications are 12.0 per cent, 12.7 per cent, 4.7 per cent, 5.3 per cent and 9.3 per cent respectively. Among the respondents with Technical Educational Qualifications (56.0 per cent only technical qualification and 4.7 per cent are having technical and graduation or more general qualification), the distribution is ITI (33.3 per cent), Diploma (8.7 per cent) B Tech/Graduation (16.0 per cent), MCA (0.07 per cent) and M.Tech. (2.0 per cent). Majority of the respondents are with technical qualifications as the firm is in the business of building of ships. The table 5.7 shows the details.

Table 5.6 Castes - Religion

Caste	Religion			Total
	Hindu	Christian	Muslim	
General	114	6	6	126
	42.5%	25.0%	75.0%	42.0%
Backward Castes	98	6	2	106
	36.6%	25.0%	25.0%	35.3%
Schedule Castes	38	8	0	46
	14.2%	33.3%		15.3%
Schedule Tribes	18	4	0	22
	6.7%	16.7%		7.3%
Total	268	24	8	300
Per cent within Religion	100.0%	100.0%	100.0%	100.0%

Table 5.7   Education

Education	Respondents
Technical Qualifications	168 (56.0%)
Within Non-Technical Qualification:	
Below SSC	
SSC/10th	28 (9.3%)
Inter	16 (5.3%)
Graduate	14 (4.7%)
Post-Graduate	38(12.7%)
Research Degrees	36(12.0%)
	0 (0.0%)
Total	
	300 (100.0%)
Non-Technical Qualification	118 (39.3%)
Within Technical Qualification:	
ITI	
Diploma	100 (33.3%)
B.Tech/Graduation	26 (8.7%)
MCA	48 (16.0%)
M.Tech.	2 (0.7%)
Research Degree	6 (2.0%)
	0 (0.0%)
Total	
	300(100.0%)

EMPLOYMENT FACTORS:

Nature of Work and Educational Qualifications: In the unit, 39.3 per cent of the respondents are having non- technical qualifications, 56.0 per cent technical qualifications and 4.7 per cent both types of qualifications. Whereas, the data shows 63.3 per cent are employed in Technical work and 36.7 per cent in non-technical work. Hence, 2.6 per cent with non-technical qualifications are engaged on technical work. The details of analysis are referred in the table 5.8.

Table 5.8   Nature of work

Type	Nature of Work	Educational Qualification
Technical	190 (63.3%)	118 (39.3%)
Non-Technical	110 (36.7%)	168 (56.0%)
Both	-	14 (4.7%)
Total	300 (100.0%)	300 (100.0%)

The cross analysis of education with nature of work reveal interesting facts. The education is tested with general education and technical education separately with nature of work. Among General Education group, nearly 3.3 per cent with

below SSC level are employed on technical work. Further, within the respondents possessing general qualifications SSC/10th (3.3 per cent), Intermediate (0.7 per cent), graduation (0.7 per cent) and post graduation (0.7 per cent) are allotted technical work. Again, respondents with technical qualifications such as ITI (1.3 per cent), Diploma (1.3 per cent), MCA (0.7 per cent) and M. Tech. (0.7 per cent) are deployed on non-technical works. The results of Education (General) with Nature of Work and Education (Technical) with Nature of Work are shown in table 5.9 and 5.10.

Classification: The manpower classification in Shipbuilding unit among the respondents shows workman as 26.7 per cent, staff as 48.0 per cent and executives as 25.3 per cent. The respondents were distributed into the following specialized activities, Engineering and Allied Services (55.3 per cent), Administration and Management (30.0 per cent), Fire and Security (5.3 per cent) and Medical (9.3 per cent). Within the specialization Engineering and Allied Services 33.7 per cent are workmen, 32.5 per cent are Staff and 33.7 per cent are Executives. And within Administration and Management 6.7 per cent are workmen, 73.3 per cent are Staff and

20.0 per cent are Executives. Further, within Fire and Security, 12.5 per cent are Workmen and 87.5 per cent are Staff. Lastly, within Medical 57.1 per cent are Workmen, 37.5 per cent are Staff and 7.1 per cent are Executives. The table 5.11 gives the description of the data.

Table 5.9 Education (General) - Nature of Work

Education (General)	Nature of Work		Total
	Technical	Non-Technical	
Below SSC	10	18	28
Per cent within nature of work	5.3%	16.4%	9.3%
Per cent of Total	3.3%	6.0%	9.3%
SSC/10th	10	6	16
Per cent within nature of work	5.3%	5.5%	5.3%
Per cent of Total	3.3%	2.0%	5.3%
Inter	2	12	14
Per cent within nature of work	1.1%	10.9%	4.7%
Per cent of Total	0.7%	4.0%	4.7%
Graduate	2	36	38
Per cent within nature of work	1.1%	32.7%	12.7%
Per cent of Total	0.7%	12.0%	12.7%
Post Graduate	2	34	36
Per cent within nature of work	1.1%	30.9%	12.0%
Per cent of Total	0.7%	11.3%	12.0%
Tech. Qualifications	164	4	168
Per cent within nature of work	86.3%	3.6%	56.0%
Per cent of Total	54.7%	1.3%	56.0%
Total	190	110	300
Per cent within nature of work	100.0%	100.0%	100.0%
Per cent of Total	63.3%	36.7%	100.0%

Table 5.10 Education (Technical) - Nature of Work

Education (Technical)	Nature of Work		Total
	Technical	**Non-Technical**	
Non-Technical Qualification	20	98	118
Per cent within nature of work	10.5%	89.1%	39.3%
Per cent of Total	6.7%	32.7%	39.3%
ITI	96	4	100
Per cent within nature of work	50.5%	3.6%	33.3%
Per cent of Total	32.0%	1.3%	33.3%
Diploma	22	4	26
Per cent within nature of work	11.6%	3.6%	8.7%
Per cent of Total	7.3%	1.3%	8.7%
B Tech /Graduation in Engineering	48	0	48
Per cent within nature of work	25.3%		16.0%
Per cent of Total	16.0%		16.0%
MCA	0	4	4
Per cent within nature of work		1.8%	0.7%
Per cent of Total		0.7%	0.7%
M Tech.	4	2	6
Per cent within nature of work	2.1%	1.8%	2.0%
Per cent of Total	1.3%	0.7%	2.0%
Total	190	110	300
Per cent within nature of work	100.0%	100.0%	100.0%
Per cent of Total	63.3%	36.7%	100.0%

Table 5.11   Classifications – Specialization

Classification	Specialization				
	Engineering Allied Services	Administration &Management	Fire & Security	Medical	Total
Workmen	56	6	2	16	80
% within classification	70.0%	7.5%	2.5%	20.0%	100.0%
%within specialization	33.7%	6.7%	12.5%	57.1%	26.7%
%within total	18.7%	2.0%	0.7%	5.3%	26.7%
Staff	54	66	14	10	144
% within classification	37.5%	45.8%	9.7%	6.9%	100.0%
%within specialization	32.5%	73.3%	87.5%	37.5%	48.0%
%within total	18%	22.0%	4.7%	3.3%	48.0%
Executive	56	18	0	2	76
% within classification	73.7%	23.7%		2.6%	100.0%
%within specialization	33.7%	20.0%		7.1%	25.3%
%within total	18.7%	6.0%		0.7%	25.3%
Total	166	90	16	28	300
% within classification	55.3%	30.0%	5.3%	9.3%	100.0%
%within specialization	100.0%	100.0%	100.0%	100.0%	100.0%
%within total	55.3%	30.0%	5.3%	9.3%	100.0%

Classification - Gender: In the unit, the classification distribution within the male respondents" follows as workman (30.6 per cent), staff (44.4 per cent) and executives (25.0 per cent). And, within the female respondents" distribution follows as workman (16.7 per cent), staff (57.1 per cent) and executives (26.2 per cent). The Pearsons chi-square coefficient value shows a significant association between classification and gender. The details follow in table 5.12.

SERVICE:

The respondents profile is analyzed for their length of service and promotion. The length of service shows the extent of attachment the employee has with the organization and job security. The promotion details give the career growth of the employee in the organization.

Length of service: In the shipbuilding unit, 17.5 per cent are having below 5 years experience, 14.7 per cent are having 5 - 10 years experience, 4.0 per cent are having 10 - 15 years experience, 9.3 per cent are having 15 - 20 years experience, 11.3 per cent are having 20 - 25 years experience, 22.0 per cent are having 25 – 30 years experience and 21.3 per cent are having above 30 years experience. Majority (54.6 per cent) of the employees are having more than 20 years of service. Further, 32.0 per cent are having less than 10 years of service and 13.3 per cent between 10 to 20 years of service. The length of service in the shipbuilding unit is high (18.6 years). The table 5.13 follows with details.

Table 5.12   Classification - Gender   **Table 5.13   Length of service**

Classification	Gender		Total
	Male	Female	
Workmen	66	14	80
	30.6%	16.7%	26.7%
Staff	96	48	144
	44.4%	57.1%	48.0%
Executives	54	22	76
	25.0%	26.2%	25.3%
Total	216	84	300
	100.0%	100.0%	100.0%

Number of years of service	Number of Respondents
Below 5	54(17.3%)
5-10	44(14.7%)
10-15	12(04.0%)
15-20	28(09.3%)
20-25	34(11.3%)
25-30	66(22.0%)
Above 30	64(21.3%)
Total	300(100.0%)

Pearsons Chi-Square: Value 3.220, Degrees of freedom 2, P-Value .200

Promotion: The promotion mix analysis in shipbuilding unit is uniform. The maximum number of 6 promotions was achieved by negligible 0.7 per cent. Further one, two, three, four and five promotions in that order were obtained by 20.0 per cent, 28.7 per cent, 18 per cent, 8.0 per cent and 1.3 per cent respectively. Nearly, 23.3 per cent of the respondents have nil promotions. In the unit gender wise, out of the male respondents a maximum of six promotions were obtained by 0.9 per cent whereas 29.6 per cent obtained three promotions and 29.6 per cent has obtained nil promotions. Similarly, out of the female respondents 47.6 per cent have attained one promotion only. Whereas 7.1 per cent, 26.2 per cent,7.1 per cent, 9.5 per cent,2.4 per cent and nil per cent of the female respondents have obtained nil, two, three, four, five and six promotions respectively. The table 5.14 follows with details.

Salary: The salary earnings per month in the shipbuilding unit ranges from below Rs. 10,000/- to above Rs. 50,000/-. Nearly 48.6 per cent are drawing less than Rs. 20,000/- per month , 28.0 per cent between Rs.20,000/- to Rs. 30,000/-, 16.0 per cent between Rs. 30,000 to Rs. 40,000 , 6.7 per cent between Rs. 40,000/- to Rs. 50,000/- and 0.7 per cent above Rs. 50,000/-.The mean for the sample is 2.57. Further, to identify gender discrimination in salary, gender data on salary is analyzed. Within the male respondents 47.2 per cent are drawing less than Rs. 20,000/-, 44.4 per cent between Rs. 20,000/ to Rs. 40,000/- and 8.3 per cent above Rs. 40,000/-. But within the female respondents 52.4 per cent are drawing less than Rs.20,000/- , 42.8 per cent between Rs. 20,000/- to Rs. 40,000/- and 4.8 per cent above Rs. 40,000/-. This shows females are in comparatively lower positions than male. The data pertaining to the above discussion is in the table 5.15.

Classification – Education: The classification of the respondents according to education reveals that 65.11 per cent, 39.1 per cent and 76.3 per cent of the respondents with technical qualifications are from workmen, staff and executive cadre respectively. Further, 27.9%, 55% and 23.7% of workmen, staff and executives" possess non-technical qualifications respectively. The remaining 3% and 4% of the workmen and staff possess both the technical and non-technical qualifications. The table 5.16 gives the details.

Gender-Specialization: The specialization wise distribution within males in descending order follows with Engineering and Allied Services (65.7 per cent), Administration and Management (26.9 per cent), Fire and Security (4.6 per cent) and Medical (2.8 per cent). And within females, the order is Administration and Management (38.1 per cent), Engineering and Allied Services (28.6 per cent), Medical (26.2 per cent) and Fire and Security (7.1 per cent). The Pearsons coefficient shows a significant association between gender and specialization. The table 5.17 provides the necessary details.

Table 5.14 Promotions - Gender

Number of Promotions	Gender		Total
	Male	Female	
0	64 (29.6%)	6 (7.1%)	70 (23.3%)
1	20 (9.3%)	40 (47.6%)	60 (20.0%)
2	64 (29.6%)	22 (29.2%)	86 (28.7%)
3	48 (22.2%)	6 (7.1%)	54 (18.0%)
4	16 (7.4%)	8 (9.5%)	24 (8.0%)
5	2 (0.9%)	2 (2.4%)	4 (1.3%)
6	2 (0.9%)	0	2 (0.7%)
Total	216 (100.0%)	84(100.0%)	300 (100.0%)
Per cent within gender			

Table 5.15   Salary - Gender

Salary in Rupees	Gender		Total
	Male	Female	
Below 10000	56	20	76
	25.9%	23.8%	25.3%
10000-20000	46	24	70
	21.3%	28.6%	23.3%
20000-30000	64	20	84
	29.6%	23.8%	28.0%
30000-40000	32	16	68
	14.8%	19.0%	16.0%
40000-50000	16	4	20
	7.4%	4.8%	6.7%
Above 50000	2	0	2
	0.9%		0.7%
Total	216	84	300
	100.0%	100.0%	100.0%

Table 5.16   Education – Classification

Education	Classification			Total
	Work-men	Staff	Exe-cutive	
Non-Technical Qualification	24	76	18	118
	27.9%	55.0%	23.7%	39.3%
Technical Qualification	56	54	58	168
	65.11%	39.1%	76.3%	56.0%
Both	6	8	0	14
	7.0%	5.8%		4.7%
Total	86	138	76	300
	100%	100%	100%	100%

Table 5.17   Specialization - Gender

Specialization	Gender		Total
	Male	Female	
Engineering & Allied Services	142 65.7%	24 28.6%	166 55.3%
Adm. & Management	58 26.9%	32 38.1%	90 30.0%
Fire & Security	10 4.6%	6 7.1%	16 5.3%
Medical	6 2.8%	22 26.2%	28 9.3%
Total	216 100.0%	84 100.0%	300 100.0%

Pearsons Chi-Square: Value 26.943, Degrees of freedom 3, P-Value .000

Classification - Nature of Work: The respondents in the shipbuilding unit within the technical group are workman (33.7 per cent), staff (35.8 per cent) and executive (30.5 per cent). Majority (69.1 per cent) of the Staff are engaged in non-technical work. Further, within non-technical group 14.5 per cent are workman, 69.1 per cent are staff and 16.4 per cent are executives. The Pearson"s chi-square coefficient and P-Value shows a significant association between classification and nature of work. The details are shown in the table 5.18.

Table 5.18 Classifications - Nature of Work

Classification	Nature of Work		Total
	Technical	Non-Technical	
Workman	64	16	80
	33.7%	14.5%	26.7%
Staff	68	76	144
	35.8%	69.1%	48.0%
Executive	58	18	76
	30.5%	16.4%	25.3%
Total	190	110	300
	100.0%	100.0%	100.0%

Pearsons Chi-Square: Value 15.591, Degrees of freedom 2, P-Value .000

Interpretation:

The mean age (45.53 years) of the shipbuilding workers in a public sector is high. The male are employed in majority and females are present in maximum (32.4 per cent) in the age group 40-50 years. The caste representation is proportionate to population distribution and the general category is high in both males" and females" group.

Further, all the caste categories are adequately represented. The females (57.1 per cent) with non-technical qualifications are more whereas men (67.6 per cent) are more with technical qualifications. Being a shipbuilding unit, majority are having technical qualifications (56.0 per cent). The interesting fact in the study is some non-technical qualified persons are engaged in technical work and vice-versa. The non-nativity factor is high and the highest is from female group (59.5 per cent). The religion affinity is favorable to the major religion Hindu (89.3 per cent) followed by Christians.

The Classification of employees" show females (57.1 per cent) are more in Staff category. Since it is Engineering Company we find more employees in Engineering and Allied Services. The mean for length of service is high (18.6 years) and it is attributed to job security in the public sector.

The promotion pattern shows disparity in comparison of males with females. The data shows male obtained more promotions then females. The mean for earnings is 2.57 and women are earning less than men. A sizable possess ITI plus B.Tech/Engineering or Diploma plus B.Tech/Engineering and additional degrees in social sciences, management etc. The trend of acquiring higher qualifications may be for better opportunities and growth, the same conditions persists in the organization. The specialization distribution reveals men as more in Engineering and Allied Services whereas women are more in Administration and Medical Services.

Chapter 6

Analysis of Organizational Climate

Organizational Climate:

The Organizational Climate is a function of number of factors. These factors are made up of criteria. Each criterion is evaluated on a Likert style five point scale. This scale is accepted as a standard format in social survey research. Each criterion is presented with five options i) strongly agree ii) agree iii) can"t say iv) disagree v) strongly disagree. The response to each criterion is chosen by the respondent based on his choice. The response towards the criteria is perception of the individual. The summation of the response is the overall prevailing attitude towards the organization. In social science research we apply two methods

i) Summation   ii) Critical Incident

The summation is the commutation of the perceptions of the end recipients. In the present analysis summation method is applied.

The factors of organizational climate are subjected to mean analysis. The analysis is shown in the following lines.

1. Objectivity and Rationality:

The perception of the employees on Objectivity and Rationality in the policies followed in the shipbuilding unit is reasonable (3.47). Nearly, 58.76 per cent of the respondents have agreed that there is objectivity and rationality in the organizations policies and procedures. About 38 per cent has felt that activities other than work are given more importance and the criterion has a mean of 3.19. The neutrality position is low (13.80 per cent) in this factor. However, majority agreed with the criterion that organization provides environment to learn (Mean: 3.55). The table 6.1 gives the details.

2. Compensation:

The compensation is paid in two forms 1) monetary terms and 2) non-monetary terms. The compensation is the inducement for employee to perform. The monetary compensation being wages, allowances, fringe benefits and perks. The non-monetary benefits may be classified as recognition, appreciation, accommodation etc. The compensation results show divergence with 46.67 per cent agreeing and 30.67 disagreeing. Further, 4.22 per cent are not satisfied with compensation. The mean (3.22) is reasonable and moderate. The neutrality within the respondents for this factor is low (11.33 per cent). The details are shown in the table 6.2.

Table 6.1   Mean Values of Objectivity & Rationality (Figures in the bracket are percentages)

Questions in Order	Strongly Disagree	Disagree	Can't Say	Agree	Strongly Agree	Total	Mean
9.The activities other than work are given more importance	34 (11.3)	118 (39.3)	34 (11.3)	100 (33.3)	14 (4.7)	300 (100)	3.19
22.The autonomy given at work is adequate	16 (5.3)	28 (9.3)	62 (20.7)	192 (64)	2 (0.7)	300 (100)	3.45
25.The organization provides environment to learn	2 (0.7)	66 (22.0)	30 (10.0)	168 (56.0)	34 (11.3)	300 (100)	3.55
26.The leadership provided by the management is good	20 (6.7)	40 (13.3)	38 (12.7)	178 (59.3)	24 (8.0)	300 (100)	3.48
28.The delega-tion of authority is adequate	8 (5.3)	32 (30.7)	56 (13.3)	200 (50.7)	4 (0)	300 (100)	3.53
32.The HR prac-tices are good	18 (6.0)	36 (12.0)	30 (10.0)	200 (66.7)	16 (5.3)	300 (100)	3.53
33. The philosophy of the organization is good.	12 (4.0)	34 (11.3)	40 (13.3)	196 (65.3)	18 (6.0)	300 (100)	3.58
Total	110 (5.24)	354 (16.85)	290 (13.80)	1234 (58.76)	112 (5.33)	2100 (100)	3.47

Table 6.2   Mean Values of Compensation   (Figures in the bracket are percentages)

Questions in Order	Strongly Disagree	Disagree	Can't Say	Agree	Strongly Agree	Total	Mean
16.Salary paid is fair	8 (2.7)	66 (22.0)	28 (9.3)	158 (52.7)	40 (13.3)	300 (100)	3.52
17.Salary is linked to perceived performance	14 (4.7)	158 (39.3)	34 (11.3)	110 (36.7)	24 (8.0)	300 (100)	3.04
18.Non-monetary rewards are good	16 (5.3)	92 (30.7)	40 (13.3)	152 (50.7)	0 (0)	300 (100)	3.09
Total	38 (4.22)	276 (30.67)	102 (11.33)	420 (46.67)	64 (7.11)	900 (100)	3.22

3. Grievance Handling:

Grievance occurs due to unsolved problems, timely solving of grievance leads to healthy organizational climate.

The Mean is 3.49 and majority of the respondent employees have reasonably accepted the factor. Nearly, 60 per cent of the sample respondents have agreed that grievance handling is acceptable. However, 14.7 per cent disagreed and 22.0 per cent were neutral to the factor. The table 6.3 shows the details.

Table 6.3 Mean Values of Grievance Handling (Figures in the bracket are percentages)

Questions in Order	Strongly Disagree	Disagree	Can't Say	Agree	Strongly Agree	Total	Mean
27.The working of grievance redressal system is acceptable	8 (2.7)	36 (12.0)	66 (22.0)	180 (60.0)	10 (3.3)	300 (100)	3.49

4. Working Conditions:

The working conditions are the overall working environment in which the employee works. These working conditions are related to health, safety and welfare at work.

The employees are satisfied with the working conditions, 52.13 per cent of the respondents agreed with the criteria on working conditions. A small per- centage (5.60 per cent) strongly disagreed with the criteria on working conditions. The mean of 3.44 shows reasonable number of employees are satisfied with working conditions. The two criteria on physical environment and outdated equipment have a moderate mean (3.2).But, 78.7 per cent are satisfied with facilities provided at work. And 81.3 per cent agree with the criterion on proper maintenance of working conditions. Nearly, 13.33 per cent has remained neutral. The details are provided in the table 6.4.

Table 6.4

Mean Values of Working Conditions

(Figures in the bracket are percentages)

Questions in Order	Strongly Disagree	Disagree	Can't Say	Agree	Strongly Agree	Total	Mean
1.All the necessary facilities for work are provided	6 (2.0)	32 (10.7)	26 (8.7)	224 (74.7)	12 (4.0)	300 (100)	3.68
2. Working conditions are properly maintained	2 (0.7)	28 (9.3)	26 (8.7)	216 (72.0)	28 (9.3)	300 (100)	3.80
3.The physical environment is bad	28 (9.3)	130 (43.3)	30 (10.0)	98 (32.7)	14 (4.7)	300 (100)	3.2
7.The equipment provided is outdated	34 (11.34)	104 (34.67)	60 (20.0)	92 (30.67)	10 (3.34)	300 (100.0)	3.2
8.The equipment provided are sophisticated	14 (4.7)	60 (20.0)	58 (19.3)	152 (50.7)	16 (5.3)	300 (100)	3.32
Total	84 (5.60)	354 (23.60)	200 (13.33)	782 (52.13)	80 (5.34)	1500 (100)	3.44

5. Performance Management:

Performance is the outcome of work, managing this performance in effective way gives good results and which in turn nurtures healthy climate. Majority of the employees have agreed to the criteria relating to performance management (54.27). Further, 9.73 per cent strongly agreed, 3.73 per cent strongly disagreed, 17.47 per cent disagreed and 14.80 per cent has remained neutral. The mean for the performance management is 3.48. The respondents to the extent of 61.3 per cent have agreed that work performance is evaluated properly. But, 24 per cent either disagreed or strongly disagreed with the criterion that the environment is conducive to achieve targets with least supervision. The respondents negated (mean 2.98) that it is difficult to achieve set targets. The strong pulling criterion is the feedback on work with a mean of 3.91. The results are given in the table 6.5.

6. Training and Development:

Training means imparting new specific skills to the employees. Development involves preparing the employee for future positions in the organization.

The mean of 3.44 shows training and development aspects are reasonably acceptable to the employees in the shipbuilding unit. Nearly, 11.3 per cent strongly agreed, 52.7 per cent agreed and 12 per cent has remained neutral. But, 7.3 per cent has strongly disagreed and 16.7 per cent disagreed with the criteria. The table 6.6 provides the details.

7. Communication:

The communication is the flow of information horizontally and vertically in the organization.

Nearly, 50 per cent has agreed to the criteria on communication as good and effective. Further, 26.22 per cent of the respondents did not accept the criteria and 17.56 per cent have remained neutral. The mean of 3.32 as seen in the table 6.7 shows the communication system in the organization is moderate. The mean (3.11) of the criterion on individual suggestions being given due weightage is moderate with 22 per cent neutral response. Further, 56.6 per cent either agree or strongly agree with effectiveness of the decision making system.

Table 6.5

Mean Values of Performance Management

(Figures in the bracket are percentages)

Questions in Order	Strongly Disagree	Disagree	Can't Say	Agree	Strongly Agree	Total	Mean
10.The work performance is evaluated properly	8 (2.7)	42 (14.0)	36 (12.0)	184 (61.3)	30 (10.0)	300 (100)	3.62
11.In the given environment one can achieve targets with least supervision	2 (0.7)	70 (23.3)	58 (19.3)	146 (48.7)	24 (8.0)	300 (100)	3.4
12. Performance targets set are difficult to achieve	24 (8.0)	92 (30.7)	56 (18.7)	112 (37.3)	16 (5.3)	300 (100)	2.98
14.The feedback on work is good	6 (2.0)	14 (4.7)	34 (11.3)	192 (64.0)	54 (18.0)	300 (100)	3.91
15.Merit and efficiency are given necessary weightage	16 (5.3)	44 (14.7)	38 (12.7)	180 (60.0)	22 (7.3)	300 (100)	3.49
Total	56 (3.73)	262 (17.47)	222 (14.80)	814 (54.27)	146 (9.73)	1500 (100)	3.48

Table 6.6   Mean Values of Training and Development

(Figures in the bracket are percentages)

Questions in Order	Strongly Disagree	Disagree	Can't Say	Agree	Strongly Agree	Total	Mean
23.The training and develop-ment given in the organi-zation is good	22 (7.3)	50 (16.7)	36 (12.0)	158 (52.7)	34 (11.3)	300 (100)	3.44

Table 6.7   Mean Values of Communications

(Figures in the bracket are percentages)

Questions in Order	Strongly Disagree	Disagree	Can't Say	Agree	Strongly Agree	Total	Mean
20. Individual suggestions are given due weightage	6 (2.0)	98 (32.7)	66 (22.0)	116 (38.7)	14 (4.7)	300 (100)	3.11
21.The decision making system is highly effective	10 (3.3)	58 (19.3)	62 (20.7)	154 (51.3)	16 (5.3)	300 (100)	3.36
24.The communication system is good	16 (5.3)	48 (16.0)	30 (10.0)	180 (60.0)	26 (8.7)	300 (100)	3.50
Total	32 (3.55)	204 (22.67)	158 (17.56)	225 (50.0)	56 (6.22)	900 (100)	3.32

8. Welfare:

The welfare provisions to the employees generally develop him mentally and morally. The analysis of the perception of the employees reveal that 69.3 per cent agree that welfare facilities are good, 16.7 per cent of the respondents disagreed with the criterion and 8.7 per cent remained neutral. The welfare provisions are agreed as satisfactory (Mean 3.58).Further, details are given in the table 6.8.

Table 6.8

Mean Values of Welfare

(Figures in the bracket are percentages)

Questions in Order	Strongly Disagree	Disagree	Can't Say	Agree	Strongly Agree	Total	Mean
31.The welfare facilities are good	14 (4.7)	36 (12.0)	26 (8.7)	208 (69.3)	16 (5.3)	300 (100)	3.58

9. Relations:

The inter-intra individual relations and the inter-intra group relations are to be woven and inter-twined. The manifestations of this relationship create an impact on the organization as a whole.

The work control by the superiors was found to be good as 62.7 per cent of the respondents have agreed to the criterion and has moderate mean (3.53). The external influence on rewards selection exists to some extent (mean: 3.17). However, 62.7 per cent of the sample has felt management does behave responsibly and 7.3 per cent strongly agree with the same.

Nearly, 78 per cent felt there is work coordination (mean: 3.68).Finally, on the whole 63.2 per cent either agree or strongly agree with the factor and 39.11 per cent disagree or strongly disagree with the factor. However the mean is moderate with 6.9.

The table 6.9 gives the referral data.

Table 6.9   Mean Values of Relations

(Figures in the bracket are percentages)

Questions in Order	Strongly Disagree	Disagree	Can't Say	Agree	Strongly Agree	Total	Mean
13.The superiors control over the subordinates work	14 (4.7)	40 (13.3)	38 (12.7)	188 (62.7)	20 (6.7)	300 (100)	3.53
19.Inter- personal connections influence rewards than efficiency	24 (8.0)	114 (38.0)	56 (18.7)	102 (34.0)	4 (1.3)	300 (100)	3.17
29.The mana-gement behaves responsible	12 (4.0)	28 (9.3)	50 (16.7)	188 (62.7)	22 (7.3)	300 (100)	3.61
30.Work coor-dination is satisfactory	6 (2.0)	26 (8.7)	34 (11.3)	224 (74.7)	10 (3.3)	300 (100)	3.68
Total	56 (4.7)	208 (17.3)	178 (14.8)	702 (58.5)	56 (4.7)	1200 (100)	3.49

10. Job design:

Job design describes and defines the job. The Job design gives the scope of work, pressure in the job and pleasure in the job.

The Job design is agreed as good by 45.11 per cent of the respondents. But, 35.6 per cent has expressed disagreement with the criteria on Job design. The mean as shown in the table 6.10 is just above the average level (2.99).

Comparing with other factors, Job design shows average response. On critical analysis of the data, 2.7 per cent strongly agree, 52.7 per cent agree, 14.0 per cent remained neutral and 30.6 per cent either disagree or strongly disagree that the work is routine without pressure. The mean (2.90) of the criterion that work load is heavy is above average. The low mean (2.82) of the criterion on work given is not adequate, justify the responses to the other criteria.The table 6.10 gives the details. The table 6.11 shows the means of the Organizational Climate factors.

Table 6.10

Mean Values of Job design

(Figures in the bracket are percentages)

Questions in Order	Strongly Disagree	Disagree	Can't Say	Agree	Strongly Agree	Total	Mean
4.The work is routine without pressure	10 (3.3)	82 (27.3)	42 (14.0)	158 (52.7)	8 (2.7)	300 (100)	3.24
5.The work load is heavy	10 (3.3)	108 (36.0)	38 (12.7)	130 (43.3)	14 (4.7)	300 (100)	2.9
6.The work given is not adequate	20 (6.7)	122 (40.7)	62 (20.7)	82 (27.3)	14 (4.7)	300 (100)	2.82
Total	40 (4.44)	312 (34.67)	142 (15.78)	370 (41.11)	36 (4.00)	900 (100)	2.99

Table 6.11

**TABLE SHOWING THE MEANS
OF ORGANISATIONAL CLIMATE FACTORS**

Factor	Mean
Objectivity and Rationality	3.47
Compensation	3.22
Grievance Handling	3.49
Working Conditions	3.44
Performance Management	3.48
Training and Development	3.44
Communications	3.32
Welfare	3.58
Relations	3.49
Job design	2.99
Organizational Climate	**3.39**

INTRA - RELATIONSHIP ANALYSIS:

For understanding the intra - relationship between the factors of organizational climate, multiple regression model is used. The regression equation explains the cause and effect relationship and the degree of the relationship. The multiple regression analysis can be used on independent variables.

$$Y = a + bx_1 + cx_2 + dx_3 + ex_4 + fx_5 + gx_6 + hx_7 + ix_8 + jx_9 + kx_{10} + u$$

Y = Dependent Variable i.e. one of the dimension of organizational climate. X_i where i takes values from 1 to 10.

X_1 = Working Conditions

X_2 = Job design

X_3 = Performance Management

X_4 = Compensation

X_5 = Relations

X_6 = Communication

X_7 = Training & Development

X_8 = Objectivity & Rationality

X_9 = Grievance

X_{10} = Welfare

Where a, b, c, d, e, f, g, h, i, j, and k are the constants and u is the error term.

The table 6.12 below provides the details of correlation among the variables. The relationship is collinear as the diagonal of the matrix is unity whereas all other values range from 0.026 to 0.517. The variables are independent.

Table 6.12
CORRELATION MATRIX OF ORGANIZATIONAL CLIMATE DIMENSIONS

	Work-ing Condi-tions	Work De-sign	Perfor-mance Manage-ment	Com-pen-sa-tion	Rela-tions	Com-muni-catio n	Train ing Deve-lopme nt	Object i-vity & Ration-lity	Grie-vanc e	Welfare
Work-ing Condi-tions	1.00									
Work Design	.133	1.00								
Perfor-mance Manage-ment	.208	.042	1.00							
Compen-sation	.072	.050	.262	1.00						
Rela-tions	.236	.032	.160	.114	1.00					
Commu-nication	.195	.174	.244	.217	.347	1.00				
Training & Deve-lopment	.253	.067	.211	.339	.268	.486	1.00			
Objecti-vity & Rationa-lity	.247	.042	.341	.454	.458	.408	.517	1.00		
Grie-vance	.385	.111	.400	.214	.257	.476	.435	.434	1.00	
Welfare	.213	-.026	.155	.421	.357	.196	.509	.530	.386	1.00

ONE ORGANIZATIONAL CLIMATE FACTOR ON OTHER ORGANIZATIONAL CLIMATE FACTORS

The organizational climate is the perception of employees towards Working Conditions, Job design, Performance Management, Compensation, Relations, Communications, Training & Development, Objectivity & Rationality, Grievance and Welfare. The summation of perceptions explains the organizational climate.

The employee perception on working conditions as dependent variable and its relation with other factors is tested with multiple regression models. The data on Working Conditions is regressed with other factors of Organizational Climate. The Working Conditions is a dependent variable and other factors of organizational climate are independent variables. The result shows only Grievance is significant and positively influencing the working conditions. The explanatory power of the equation R^2 is .191 i.e. 19.1 per cent of variance is explained. The F-test is significant suggesting appropriateness of the model.

In the next step, Job design as dependent variable is regressed with other factors of organizational climate. The other factors are independent variables. The analysis shows none of the variables are significantly influencing Job design. The explanatory power (R^2) is .051.

The Performance Management as dependent variable is regressed on other independent variables. The Grievance, Objectivity & Rationality and Compensation are found to be influencing Performance Management. The explanation power of R^2 is .227 i.e. 22.7 per cent of the explanation of the variance. When regression model is tested with Compensation as dependent variable and other factors of organizational climate as independent variables, Performance Management, Relations, Objectivity & Rationality and Welfare were found as influencing variables whereas the impact of Relations is negative. The explanatory power of the model (R^2) is .303 i.e. 30.3 per cent of explanation.

The Relations as dependent variable is regressed with other independent variables. It was found Communication, Objectivity & Rationality and Welfare are positively influencing while Compensation is negatively influencing. The explanatory power is .301. Further, F-test is significant suggesting appropriateness of the model. The explanatory variable when Communication is regressed with other variables is (R^2) 0.410 (41.0 per cent). The factors positively influencing are found to be Relations, Training & Development and Grievance. Whereas, Welfare is influencing the dependent variable negatively.

The Training & Development as a dependent variable is regressed with other independent variables. The Communication, Objectivity & Rationality and Welfare are influencing positively. The explanation accounts for 45.4 per cent (R^2 : .454). In the next step, Objectivity & Rationality as dependent variable is regressed with other organizational climate variables. The Performance Management, Compensation, Relations, Training & Development and Welfare are positively influencing and the explanation accounts for 51.8 per cent i.e. R^2: .518· The Grievance is positively influenced by Working Conditions, Performance Management, Communication and Welfare. The Grievance as dependent variable and other variables as independent variables has an explanatory power R^2 as 0.442 i.e. 44.2 per cent. The model when tested with F- test was found to be significant.

In the last step, Welfare is regressed with organizational climate variables and the explanatory power of the equation is .462. The variables found positively influencing are Compensation, Relations, Training & Development, Objectivity & Rationality and Grievance. The impact of Communication is negative on the dependent variable. The other variables are found to be insignificant. The significant values are given in the table 6.13.

Table 6.13

SIGNIFICANCE TABLE OF ONE ORGANISATIONAL CLIMATE FACTOR ON OTHER ORGANISTIONAL CLIMATE FACTORS

Dependent Organizational Climate Variable	Significant Independent Organizational Climate Variable	R^2	t Value
1.Working Conditions	1.Grievance	.191	3.055*
2.Job design	None	.051	--
3.Performance Management	1.Compensation 2.Objectivity & Rationality 3.Grievance	.227	1.967*** 1.853*** 3.386*
4.Compensation	1.Performance Management 2.Relations 3.Objectivity & Rationality 4.Welfare	.303	1.967*** -1.977*** 3.226* 3.223*
5. Relations	1.Compensation 2.Communication 3. Objectivity & Rationality 4. Welfare	.301	-1.977*** 2.866* 3.658* 2.623**

Continued in the next page

Dependent Organizational Climate Variable	Significant Independent Organizational Climate Variable	R^2	t Value
6.Communication	1.Relations 2. Training & Development 3. Grievance 4. Welfare	.410	2.866* 4.221* 3.833* -2.896*
7.Training & Development	1.Communication 2. Objectivity & Rationality 3.Welfare	.454	4.221* 2.250** 3.881*
8.Objectivity &Rationality	1. Performance Management 2. Compensation 3. Relations 4. Training & Development 5. Welfare	.518	1.853*** 3.226* 3.658* 2.250** 2.432**
9.Grievance	1. Working Conditions 2. Performance Management 3. Communication 4. Welfare	442	3.055* 3.386* 3.833* 2.662*
10. Welfare	1. Compensation 2. Relations 3. Communication 4. Training & Development 5. Objectivity & Rationality 6. Grievance	.462	3.223* 2.623** -2.896* 3.881* 2.432** 2..662*

Significance Levels *: 1% **: 5% ***: 10%

Interpretation:

The Organizational Climate is the perception of the employees. The Organizational Climate is the summation of the perception of the individuals towards the following factors Working Conditions, Job design, Performance Management, Compensation, Relations, Communication, Training and Development, Objectivity and Rationality, Grievance and Welfare. The Organizational Climate in the public sector shipbuilding organization is moderate (3.39). The Welfare as a factor has a high mean (3.58). The Relations (3.49), Grievance Handling (3.49) and Working Conditions (3.48) are the other factors influencing the Organizational Climate in high order. The least out of all the factors is Job design (2.99).

The intra-dimensional regression reveals that all the factors are influencing each other. However, Job design is isolated and no impact is made by any of the factors. The Welfare is influenced by six factors namely Compensation, Relations, Training and Development, Objectivity and Rationality and Grievance Handling positively and whereas by Communication negatively. The Welfare is given top priority in public sectors. The Relations, Training and Development, Objectivity and Rationality and Grievance Handling are the major contributors in formation of Organizational Climate in the organization. The existence of cordial relations, human resource practices, positive grievance solving and adequate training and development are the important contributors in providing enabling environment. However, Communication is a negative contributor. The unit has undergone financial and administrative restructuring and change in administrative control from Ministry of Surface Transport to Ministry of Defense on account of recurring losses. The transfer from commercial shipyard to defense yard has some bearing on Training and Development, Policies and Practices and Grievance Settlements.

IMPACT OF PROFILE FACTORS ON ORGANIZATIONAL CLIMATE:

Further, to understand the relationship between organizational climate factors and profile factors, multiple regressions are applied. Each factor of the organizational climate is regressed with profile factors viz., Age, Gender, Caste, Nature of Education, Nature of Work, Salary, Classification and Service. The profile factors are a combination of personal identity and employment identity.

The multiple regression model is based on the equation $Y = a + bX_1 + cX_2 + dX_3 + eX_4 + fX_5 + gX_6 + hX_7 + iX_8 + u$

Y = Dependent variable i.e. one of the factors of organizational climate. X_1 = Age

X_2 = Gender

X_3 = Caste

X_4 = Nature of Education

X_5 = Nature of Work

X_6 = Salary

X_7 = Classification

X_8 = Service

Where a, b, c, d, e, f, g, h and i are coefficients and u is the error term.

First, Working Conditions is regressed on profile variables. The explanatory power of the equation (R^2) is 0.065. The Nature of Work and Service are negatively influencing the dependent variable whereas Age is influencing positively. When Job design as dependent variable is regressed with profile variables, it was found that only Age is influencing positively. The explanatory power of the equation (R^2) is 0.123 i.e. 12.3 per cent. The F-test is significant and it may be concluded that the model is appropriate.

In the next step, Performance Management is regressed with profile variables. The explanatory power of the variable (R^2) is 0.151. The Age, Nature of Education, Nature of Work, Salary and Classification were found to be the influencing variables. The F-test is significant at 1% level, so it may be concluded that the model is acceptable. The Age, Gender, Caste, Nature of Education, Nature of Work and Classification were significant when Compensation as dependent variable is regressed with profile variables. The explanatory power of the variable (R^2) is .164. The Nature of Education and Nature of Work are negatively influencing. The Relations as dependent variable is influenced by the Nature of Education and Classification negatively. The explanatory power of the variable is .139. Next, Communication as dependent variable is regressed with other profile variables. The explanatory power of the variable (R^2) is .071, only Age was found to be influencing. In the next step, Training and Development is kept as dependent variable and regressed with other profile variables, the explanatory power (R^2) is .083. The Age was found to be influencing positively whereas Nature of Work is doing the same negatively.

When Objectivity and Rationality is regressed with other profile variables, the impact of Caste is negative. The explanatory power (R^2) of the equation is 0.077. The Grievance as dependent variable is influenced by salary negatively and the explanatory factor (R^2) is .102. Finally, when Welfare as dependent variable is regressed with profile factors, it was found Nature of Education, Nature of Work, Classification and Service are negatively significant whereas only Gender is positive and significant. The explanatory power of the equation (R^2) is .160. The significant values are given in the table 6.14.

Table 6.14
SIGNIFICANCE TABLE OF ONE ORGANISATIONAL CLIMATE FACTORS ON PROFILE FACTORS

Organizational Climate factors	Age	Gender	Caste	Profile Factors		Salary	Classifi-cation	Service
				Nature of Education	Natur eof Work			
Working Conditions	2.069*				-1.753**			-1.764***
Job design	1.668***							
Performance Management	2.515**			-1.986**	-2.443*	-3.034*	3.018*	
Compensation	2.376**	1.678***	1.666***	2.160**	2.525**		2.504**	

Relations				-1.754***			-2.849*	
Communications	2.355**							
Training and Development	2.550**				-2.198**			
Objectivity and Rationality			-2.713*					
Grievance						-2.403**		
Welfare		2.392**		-1.701***	3.597*		-1.842***	-2.006**

Significant Values: * 1 per cent , ** 5 per cent, *** 10 per cent

Interpretation: The profile factors namely Age, Gender, Caste, Nature of Education, Nature of Work, Salary, Classification and Service affect on organizational climate factors shows some interesting facts. The Age was a major influencing factor of organizational climate. The Nature of Work is an important factor acting negatively on organizational climate factors. The Welfare is a major component in organizational climate which is positively inter-twined with Gender and negatively with Nature of Education, Nature of Work, Classification and Service.

Therefore, the study reveals that in restructured Public Sector shipbuilding unit Age determines and influences the organizational climate. But, the impact of Nature of Work on organizational climate is negative.

Chapter 7

Analysis of Perceived Performance

PERCEIVED PERFORMANCE:

Perceived Performance means not simply producing more output, it is one"s perceived experience at work. Therefore, for measuring the Perceived Performance, the below 5 factors are considered.

1. Discipline

2. Job

3. Planning and Execution

4. Guidance and Counseling

5. Individuality

Further, each factor has number of criteria. Since it is a perceptional study, the employees were asked to rate their perceived performance on a 5-point scale. The respondents were to select their choice from the options a) Below Average b) Average c) Good d) Very Good e) Outstanding

1. Discipline:

Discipline refers to person"s ability to adhere to the work place rules and regulations.

In the study, 86 per cent rated themselves as good regarding adherence to discipline at the work spot. The mean of the responses is 3.42, which is moderately good and the same is shown in the table 7.1.

2. Job:

In order to perform on the job, the employee is expected to have good knowledge of the job and the ability to implement it effectively.

The self-rating on the job factor shows 12.33 per cent rated them as average and 0.7 per cent as below average. The rest of the respondents (86.97 per cent) rated their perceived performance on the job as above average. The mean value 3.34 is moderate. The details are shown in the table 7.2.

Table 7.1

Discipline
(Figures in the brackets are percentages)

Questions in Order	Below Average	Average	Good	Very Good	Outstanding	Total	Mean
3.Punctuality	0 (0.0)	40 (13.3)	108 (36.0)	130 (43.3)	22 (7.3)	300 (100)	3.44
11.Discipline	8 (2.7)	36 (12.0)	98 (32.7)	142 (47.3)	16 (5.3)	300 (100)	3.40
Total	8 (1.33)	76 (12.67)	206 (34.33)	272 (45.33)	38 (6.34)	600 (100)	3.42

Table 7.2

Job

(Figures in the brackets are percentages)

Questions in Order	Below Average	Average	Good	Very Good	Outstan-ding	Total	Mean
1.Job knowledge	2 (0.7)	32 (10.7)	134 (44.7)	108 (36.0)	24 (8.0)	300 (100)	3.4
5.Effecti-veness at work	2 (0.7)	42 (14.0)	144 (48.0)	92 (30.7)	20 (6.7)	300 (100)	3.28
Total	4 (0.7)	74 (12.33)	278 (46.33)	200 (33.32)	44 (7.32)	600 (100)	3.34

3. Planning and Execution:

Planning is an important conceptual skill required for perceived performance. Further, execution of the conceived plan is a combination of technical skill and human resources skill. Therefore, perception of the employee on his or her performance in planning and execution of the job is collected for analysis.

The analysis shows 21.20 per cent are average or below in planning and execution, 42.53 per cent are good and 4.54 per cent rate them as outstanding. The mean of the responses is 3.16. However, a sizable number of respondents (36.7 per cent) felt a problem in foreseeing problems. A majority of them (81.3 per cent) felt good or above in achievement of targets set. The mean results can be seen in the table 7.3.

4. Guidance and Counseling:

Guidance and Counseling is also included as criteria for rating perceived performance. The holistic approach to perceived performance is adopted for the study.

The mean response for guidance and counseling is 3.14. Nearly, 80.7 per cent of the respondents rated themselves as good and above on this aspect. Further, 19.3 per cent rated themselves as average and below average. The table 7.4 gives the details.

5. Individuality:

Individuality refers to your ability to accomplish given tasks and duties without depending on others.

About 48 per cent of the respondents rated themselves as average or below average, 50.67 per cent rated themselves as good and 1.33 per cent rated them as outstanding.

The mean of the responses is 2.62 which are just above average. The mean of 2.36 for the statement dependence on others for completing given task shows the work is based on relations and the statement on dependability for work criteria has a mean of 2.87, which shows some under rated performance. The tabulation details are shown in the table 7.6. The means of all the factors are shown in the table 7.7.

Table 7.3

Planning and Execution

(Figures in the brackets are percentages)

Questions in Order	Below Average	Average	Good	Very Good	Out-standing	Total	Mean
4.Achievement of organizational objectives	0 (0.0)	42 (14.0)	136 (45.3)	106 (35.3)	16 (5.3)	300 (100)	3.32
6.Planning your work	2 (0.7)	48 (16.0)	136 (45.3)	96 (32.0)	18 (6.0)	300 (100)	3.26
8.Decision making	18 (6.0)	52 (17.3)	122 (40.7)	96 (32.0)	12 (4.0)	300 (100)	3.10
9.Foreseeing problems	18 (6.0)	92 (30.7)	114 (38.0)	64 (21.3)	12 (4.0)	300 (100)	2.86
10.Achievement of target set	2 (0.7)	44 (14.7)	130 (43.3)	114 (38.0)	10 (3.3)	300 (100)	3.28
Total	40 (2.67)	278 (18.53)	638 (42.53)	476 (31.73)	68 (4.54)	1500 (100)	3.16

Table 7.4

Guidance and Counseling

(Figures in the brackets are percentages)

Questions in Order	Below Average	Average	Good	Very Good	Out-standing	Total	Mean
7.Guiding subordinates	10 (3.3)	48 (16.0)	150 (50.0)	74 (24.7)	18 (6.0)	300 (100)	3.14

Table 7.5

Individuality

(Figures in the brackets are percentages)

Questions in Order	Below Average	Average	Good	Very Good	Out-standing	Total	Mean
2.Dependability for work	26 (8.7)	74 (24.7)	118 (39.3)	76 (25.3)	6 (2.0)	300 (100)	2.87
12.Dependence on others	52 (17.3)	136 (45.3)	66 (22.0)	44 (14.7)	2 (0.7)	300 (100)	2.36
Total	78 (13)	210 (35)	184 (30.67)	120 (20)	8 (1.33)	600 (100)	2.62

Table 7.6

TABLE SHOWING THE MEANS
OF PERCEIVED PERFORMANCE FACTORS

Factor	Mean
1.Discipline	3.42
2.Job	3.34
3.Planning and Execution	3.16
4.Guidance and Counseling	3.14
5.Individuality	2.62
Perceived Performance	**3.14**

:

INTRA-RELATIONSHIP ANALYSIS OF PERCEIVED PERFORMANCE:

The multiple regression model $Y = a + bX_1 + cX_2 + dX_3 + eX_4 + fX_5 + u$ is applied to understand the relationship between one of the Perceived Performance factor with other Perceived Performance factors.

Where Y = dependent variable i.e. one of the factors of Perceived Performance and X_i is independent variable where $i = 1,2,3,4$ and 5

X_1 = Job

X_2 = Planning and Execution

X_3 = Guidance and Counseling

X_4 = Discipline

X_5 = Individuality

a, b, c, d, e and f are coefficients and u is the error term. The correlation matrix (table 7.7) between the factors of Perceived Performance shows positive correlation among the variable factors. The variables are independent and correlated, the diagonal column is unity and the values range from 0.064 to 0.533.

Table 7.7

CORRELATION MATRIX

	Guidance &	Individuality	Discipline	Planning &	Job
	Counseling			Execution	
Guidance & **Counseling**	1.000	.073	.064	.518	.432
Individuality	.073	1.000	.172	.090	.238
Discipline	.064	.172	1.000	.167	.203
Planning & **Execution**	.518	.090	.167	1.000	.533
Job	.432	238	.203	.533	1.000

In the first step, Job as dependent variable is regressed with other perceived performance variables, the F-test for the model is significant. The explanatory power of the equation is .360 i.e. 36.0 per cent. The Planning and Execution, Individuality and Guidance and Counseling are found to be positively influencing Job.

In the second step, Guidance and Counseling is tested by keeping it as dependent variable, the F-test was found to be significant for the model. The variables account for 30.5 per cent of the explanation i.e. R^2 is .305. The Job and Planning and Execution were found to positively influencing the dependent variable.

In the third step, the Planning and Execution as a dependent variable is regressed on the other variables of organizational climate. The F-test is significant and R^2 the explanatory power of the variable is .392, i.e. 39.2 per cent explanation. The Job and Guidance and Counseling are found to be positively influencing the dependent variable.

In the fourth step, Discipline as a dependent variable is regressed with other perceived performance factors as independent variables. The F- test on the model is significant at 5 per cent level and the explanatory power of the variables is .066. Further, none of the independent variables were found to be significant.

Finally, Individuality as dependent variable is regressed on the other variables of perceived performance. The F- test of the model was found to be significant at 5 per cent level. The explanatory power of the variables is .076 i.e. 7.6 per cent. Only, Job variable was found to be influencing positively whereas other variables are insignificant. The significance level of one perceived performance factor on other perceived performance factors is shown in the table 7.8.

Table 7.8

SIGNIFICANCE TABLE OF ONE PERCEIVED PERFORMANCE FACTOR ON OTHER PERCEIVED PERFORMANCE FACTORS

Dependent Perceived Performance variable	Significant Independent Perceived Performance Variable	R^2	t Value
1. Job	Planning and Execution Individuality Guidance and Counseling	.360	4.987* 2.535** 2.701*
2. Guidance and Counseling	Job Planning and Execution	.305	2.701* 4.942*
3. Planning and Execution	Job Guidance and Counseling	.392	4.987* 4.942*
4. Discipline	Nil	.066	-
5. Individuality	Job	.076	2.535**

Significance Levels *: 1% **: 5% ***: 10%

Interpretation:

Performance is measured with output, traits exhibited or behavior. The perceived performance is the perception about own work experience at the work. The perceived performance is the self-evaluation of one"s exhibited behavior at work.

The Discipline as a factor of perceived performance is a major influencing factor (3.42). The Job and Planning and Execution are the other important contributors. The Individuality (2.62) is the least contributor. The intra-dimensional factors of perceived performance are influencing one and other positively. But, Discipline is not influenced by any other factor. Therefore, Discipline is independent and correlates directly with perceived performance. The Job is significant with three independent variables Planning and Execution, Individuality and Guidance and Counseling. The perceived performance in the shipbuilding unit is moderate (3.14).

II.   **JOB SATISFACTION:**

The statistical data reveals that 68 per cent has agreed that their job gives them satisfaction, 14 per cent has strongly agreed with the statement and 7.3 per cent remained neutral. Nearly, 10.7 per cent of the respondents have replied in negative. Further, 2.7 per cent has strongly refuted the statement. The Mean also reveals the same and it is shown in the table 7.9.

Table 7.9
Job satisfaction
(Figures in the brackets are percentages)

Questions in Order	Strongly Disagree	Disagree	Can't Say	Agree	Strongly Agree	Total	Mean
34.The job provides satisfaction to me	8 (2.7)	24 (8.0)	22 (7.3)	204 (68.0)	42 (14.0)	300 (100)	3.82

IMPACTING PROFILE FACTORS ON JOB SATISFACTION:

The Job Satisfaction and its relation with profile variables are tested for association using multiple regression models. The model regression equation is

$$Y = a + bX_1 + cX_2 + dX_3 + eX_4 + fX_5 + gX_6 + hX_7 + iX_8 + u$$

Y = Dependent Variable i.e. Job Satisfaction.

X_1 = Age

X_2 = Gender

X_3 = Caste

X_4 = Nature of Education

X_5 = Nature of Work

X_6 = Salary

X_7 = Classification and

X_8 = Service

Where a, b, c, d, e, f, g, h, and i are constants and u is the error term.

The regression analysis of job satisfaction on profile variables shows that the explanatory power (R^2) is 0.067. Further, Nature of Education and Nature of Work are negatively influencing the dependent variable. The table 7.10 shows the significant factors.

Interpretation:

The Job Satisfaction has a moderately high mean (3.82). The inter-dimensional influence of job satisfaction with profile factors is negative. The job satisfaction is negatively associated with Nature of Education and Nature of Work for ship- building employees.

Table 7.10

**SIGNIFICANCE TABLE OF JOB SATISFACTION WITH
PROFILE FACTORS**

Dependent Variable	Profile Factors which are Significant	t- Value
Job Satisfaction	Nature of Education	-2.034**
	Nature of Work	-2.536**

Summary: R^2: .067

Chapter 8

Analysis of Linkage between Organizational Climate,

Perceived Performance and Job Satisfaction

RELATIONSHIP BETWEEN ORGANIZATIONAL CLIMATE, PERCEIVED PERFORMANCE AND JOB SATISFACTION:

ONE FACTOR OF PERCEIVED PERFORMANCE ON ORGANIZATIONAL CLIMATE FACTORS:

The Regression Model $Y = a + bX_1 + cX_2 + dX_3 + eX_4 + fX_5 + gX_6 + hX_7 + iX_8 + jX_9 + kX_{10} + u$

is applied to understand the relationship between each of perceived performance factors on organizational climate factors. Here, Y = Dependent Variable i.e. one of the factors of Perceived Performance. Whereas

X_1 = Working Conditions

X_2 = Job design

X_3 = Performance Management

X_4 = Compensation

X_5 = Relations

X_6 = Communication

X_7 = Training and Development

X_8 = Objectivity and Rationality

X_9 = Grievance

X_{10} = Welfare

Where a,b,c,d,e,f,g,h,i,j and k are constants and u is the error term.

First, Job is regressed with organizational climate variables. The F-test for the model is significant. The exploratory power of the equation (R^2) is .218 . The Compensation, Relations and Objectivity and Rationality were found to influencing positively while Communication is negatively influencing the dependent variable.

Second, Guidance and Counseling as a dependent variable is regressed with organizational climate variables. The F-test is significant and the explanatory power (R^2) is 0.106. The Objectivity and Rationality was found to be influencing the dependent variable positively and significantly.

Third, Planning and Execution as a dependent variable, when regressed shows the explanatory power of R^2 as 0.127.

Fourth, the regression model of Discipline as dependent variable on organizational climate variables is significant. The explanatory power (R^2) is 0.218. Then, Performance Management, Relations and Welfare are influencing the dependent variable positively and significantly.Lastly, Individuality is regressed with other organizational climate variables, The F-test is significant and the explanatory power R^2 is 0.095. Only, Job design and Relations were positively influencing the dependent variable.

Table 8.1

SIGNIFICANCE TABLE OF ONE FACTOR OF

PERCEIVED PERFORMANCE ON ORGANIZATIONAL

CLIMATE FACTORS

Dependent Perceived Performance variable	Significant Independent Organizational Climate Variables	R^2	t -Value
1.Job	1.Compensation 2.Relations 3.Communication 4.Objectivity and Rationality	.218	2.592** 1.966*** -2.593** 1.849***
2.Guidance and Counseling	1.Objectivity and Rationality	.106	3.068*
3.Planning and Execution	1.Objectivity and Rationality	.127	2.061**
4. Discipline	1.Performance Management 2.Relations 3.Welfare	.218	1.956*** 2.752* 3.062*
5.Individuality	1. Job design 2. Relations	.095	2.815* 1.729***

Significance Levels *: 1% **: 5% ***: 10%

Interpretation:

The Perceived Performance factors and Organizational Climate factors are inter-twined and affecting each other. But, negative trend is seen when Communication is tested with Job factor. The Objectivity and Rationality is a major factor in Job, Guidance and Counseling and Planning and Execution.

Further, the study establishes Job design as a major contributor to Individuality at the work for ship building employees.

JOB SATISFACTION ON ORGANIZATIONAL CLIMATE FACTORS:

In the next stage, Job Satisfaction is regressed with Organizational Climate variables the model for the equation is

$$Y = a + bX_1 + cX_2 + dX_3 + eX_4 + fX_5 + gX_6 + hX_7 + iX_8 + jX_9 + kX_{10} + u$$

Y = Dependent Variable i.e. Job Satisfaction.

X_1 = Working Conditions

X_2 = Job design

X_3 = Performance Management

X_4 = Compensation

X_5 = Relations

X_6 = Communication

X_7 = Training and Development

X_8 = Objectivity and Rationality

X_9 = Grievance

X_{10} = Welfare

Where a, b, c, d, e, f, g, h, and i are constants and u is the error term.

The regression results show that the F – test is significant and R^2 the explanatory power of the variable is .282 i.e. 28.2 per cent. The Performance Management and Objectivity and Rationality are positively significant. Therefore, these variables are positively influencing the dependent variable. The significant factors of organizational climate on job satisfaction are shown in the table 8.2.

Table 8.2

SIGNIFICANCE TABLE OF JOB SATISFACTION ON ORGANIZATIONAL CLIMATE VARIABLES

Dependent Variable	Organizational Climate Factors which are Significant	t- Value
Job Satisfaction	Performance Management	2.460**
	Objectivity and Rationality	1.723***

Summary: R^2 : .282 Significance Levels *: 1% **: 5% ***: 10%

JOB SATISFACTION ON PERCEIVED PERFORMANCE FACTORS:

Next, to find the influence of Perceived Performance factors on Job Satisfaction, the following multiple regression model is used.

$$Y = a + bX_1 + cX_2 + dX_3 + eX_4 + fX_5 + u$$

Y = Dependent Variable i.e. Job Satisfaction.

X_1 = Job

X_2 = Guidance and Counseling

X_3 = Planning and Execution

X_4 = Discipline

X_5 = Individuality

Where a, b, c, d, e and f are constants and u is the error term.

Whereas regression result shows that the F-test is significant and the explanatory power of the equation R^2 is 0.076. Further, only Discipline is positively influencing (t: 1.881, significant at 10 per cent level) the dependent variable. The result is shown in the table 8.3.

Table 8.3

SIGNIFICANCE TABLE OF PERCEIVED PERFORMANCE

FACTORS ON JOB SATISFACTION

Dependent Variable	Significant Perceived Performance Factors	t- Value
Job Satisfaction	Discipline	1.881***

Summary: R^2 : .076   Significance Levels *: 1% **: 5% ***: 10%

The relationship between Organizational Climate and Perceived Performance is also found out by regressing the organizational climate as dependent variable and perceived performance as independent variable.

The relation is tested with linear regression equation.

$Y = a + bX + u$

Y = Dependent Variable i.e. Organizational Climate

X = Independent Variable = Perceived Performance

Where a, b are coefficients and u is the error term.

The F-test is significant suggesting the efficiency of the model. The explanatory power (R^2) is .064. The perceived performance variable is significantly and positively influencing the organizational climate (3.187 *). The significance is at 1 per cent level.

In the next step, to understand the relationship between Organizational Climate and Job Satisfaction, Organizational Climate is regressed with Job Satisfaction. Here, the following linear Regression Model is applied.

$Y = a + bX + u$

Where Y= Organizational Climate i.e. the dependent variable

X = Job Satisfaction is the Independent Variable.

Further, a, b are coefficients and u is the error term.

The explanatory power of the variable (R^2) is 0.126. The relationship is significant and the dependent variable is positively influencing the organizational climate.

The relationship between perceived performance and job satisfaction is examined by applying the linear regression. In the equation $Y = a + bX + U$

Y = dependent variable i.e. Perceived Performance

X = Independent variable i.e. Job Satisfaction whereas a, b are constants and u is the error term.

The F-test for the model is significant and the explanatory power of the equation is .055. But, it is low. It was found that Job Satisfaction is positively influencing perceived performance (t: 2.941).

Interpretation:

The Performance Management and Objectivity and Rationality of the Organizational Climate are the two factors directly affecting Job Satisfaction. The Job Satisfaction and the Organizational Climate factors are intertwined and influencing each other. But, other factors are insignificant. The employees derive satisfaction as performance is evaluated and results are utilized to their satisfaction. Out of perceived performance factors, only Discipline is influencing job satisfaction.

The Job Satisfaction is a manifestation of Organizational Climate. The Organizational Climate is moderate (3.39) and the same is reflected in Job Satisfaction which is also moderate (3.82). However, only two Organizational Climate factors are intertwined significantly with Job Satisfaction. Comparatively, job satisfaction is higher than organizational climate. But, perceived performance (3.14) is lower than organizational climate. The productivity is a measure of performance, in the organization the productivity measured as man hours per dead weight tonnage has improved from 27.20 in 2009-10 to 42.5 in 2010-11 to 45 in 2011-12. Therefore, these results corroborate with perceived performance.

The Organizational Climate, Perceived Performance and Job Satisfaction are intertwined and influencing each other positively. The hypotheses are found to be true in the study. But profile factors are playing a negative role in the restructured public sector unit.

Chapter 9

Summary, Conclusion and Suggestions

SUMMARY:

The economic development of nation depends on many factors. The industrial growth and development is one such factor. The Industrial health is a prerequisite for industrial growth. The globalization era generally attract the part of the world which has been unexplored due to variety of causes. The attention is especially directed towards countries of the third world. India with its vast unexplored resources is naturally the choice of the world. Lately, India has become the destination for large Multinational Corporate firms for its vast potential market. The proximity of India as a gateway to other parts of the world has attracted manufacturers. The human resources with skill variety have been a factor to relocate the services and manufacturing base to India. The Indian Government has pursued liberalization policy with disinvestment, privatization and restructuring as its features. The Indian Policy post independence traversed from private to nationalization, and presently to privatization and private-public partnership. Presently, many areas are open for private partnership. The management practices are affected by these external factor influences. In this context, Indian economic environment has undergone changes and affected the operating environment. The public sector versus private sector competition has made many public sector business models unviable. The Government of India aided the public sector through restructuring, privatization and disinvestment (to increase capitalization). The restructuring process seeks to obtain financial leverage, structural leverage and human resources leverage.

The organization is understood as coming together of people for common purpose. It is a group of people together for common activity, a form of human association for the attainment of a common purpose. The organization defines and delegates responsibility, authority and establishes relationships for the purpose of enabling people to work most effectively together in accomplishing objectives.

The organizational behavior is studied at different levels namely, individual, role, inter and intra groups and organization. But, when the organization is the level, then the following concepts are the subject of study; organizational culture, organizational climate, organizational communication, organizational learning, organizational change, organizational development, power, politics and cross-cultures.

The organizational climate is viewed as the summation of perception which people have about an organization and it identifies the organization. Some say it is an assessment of organizational outlook, attitudes, belief, norms, values etc. The organizational climate has an impact on performance and the organizational climate is propelled by the individual behavior.

The above review of definitions view organizational climate as characteristics or attitudes or values which are prevailing in the organization. Further, the manifestations of human resource practices are these characteristics. So, measuring these characteristics with respect to a frame of reference is a significant step. The literature is contradictory with authors and researchers suggesting different methods.

The organizational climate and culture are the two concepts which attracted the attention of the theoreticians and researchers alike in the recent past. The literature on differentiation between the two terms is contradictory. Further different dimensions and approaches are used to study the concept of organizational climate.

Litwin and Stringer (1968) has used six motives, Likert (1967) proposed six dimensions and Udai Pareek (2004) examined the concept with six motives and twelve processes.

Based on review the concept of Organizational Climate is viewed as collective personality, characterized by the social and professional interactions within it, the collective behavior of personality and a phenomenon that is influenced by both the internal and external environments. Further it is durable and changes with time period. The organizational climate is the summation or averages of the shared perceptions.

Human Resource Practices are critical part of the management process. The competitive strength of the organization is its human resources. The Human Resources Practices relating to strategic orientation, staffing, compensation, human resources development and relations are internal influencing factors and makers of Organizational Culture and consequently Organizational Climate.

The Organizational Climate is a measure of identity for an organization. The Organizational Climate is a competitive factor in the world. Hamel and Prahlad (2002) say"s in today"s world, competition is for future and the competitive factor is core competencies. The organization brand is an important element in the competition. The importance of organizational climate in the present global context is its ability to provide competitive edge. The global factor has made identity a critical component for competition. The organizational climate is an important factor and a measure of healthy practices. The Human Resources Practices and Procedures nurture the culture of an organization. But unfortunately, the term organizational climate is contradictory with many definitions, demarcations and dimensions. Therefore, the corporate and business strategy is oriented by the organization to create right climate in the organization.

The manifestations of organizational climate are job satisfaction and perceived performance. The satisfaction with job creates a climate for furthering the performance. The Job Satisfaction is inherent to the organizational climate and varies. Further, the actual – expected variation influences the Job Satisfaction.

The term Perceived Performance is an experience of work as perceived by the individual. Further, the perceived performance is a subjective term. Human Resources Management practices influence the performance of employees. Anakwe (2002) suggests that human resource practices in developing countries have also been traditional and performance is the criteria.

 Keeping in view the above context, the study was conducted in Hindustan Shipyard Limited in Visakhapatnam. The post liberalization policies have financially disturbed the organization due to paucity of orders. But lately the Organization was transferred from commercial oriented ship building to defense undertaking in 2010. Further, financial structuring was done for better financial leverage. This restructuring process was implemented to overcome the problems inflicted due to transitions in economy.

The Hindustan Shipyard Limited is a public sector organization. In the initial phase it was a private sector enterprise, but later in 1962 the firm was nationalized. In the year 2010, as a part of restructuring, the firm is transferred to Ministry of Defense. Therefore, the Organization has undergone a major change.

The study was broadly divided into Organizational Climate and its manifestations namely Job Satisfaction and Perceived Performance. The main intention being to study the intra and inter dimensional linkage between profile factors, organizational climate, job satisfaction and perceived performance. The sample for the study was drawn randomly from the universe and it is 14 per cent of the universe i.e. 300. The primary data was collected from the respondents with the help of a questionnaire. The questionnaire was prepared using standard Likert style format. The questionnaire was constructed with a view to collect information pertaining to 1) Profile factors 2) Organizational Climate 3) Job Satisfaction and 4)Perceived Performance. The questions on Organizational Climate has 33 criteria and where divided into 10 factors. Further, for perceptions on Perceived Performance 12 criteria were used and where divided into 5 factors. The Job Satisfaction is collected with 1 criterion. The factors were conceptualized based on the review of literature and empirical studies. The secondary data was sourced from company manual, existing literature, empirical studies and internet. The Organizational Climate in Hindustan Shipyard Limited is estimated with the following the factors

(i)Objectivity and Rationality (ii) Compensation (iii) Grievance Handling (iv)Working Conditions (v) Performance Management (vi)Training and Development (vii) Communications (viii) Welfare (ix) Relations and (x) Job design

Similarly, the Perceived Performance in Hindustan Shipyard is estimated with the following factors i) Job ii) Guidance and Counseling iii) Planning and Execution iv) Individuality v) Discipline.

The following hypotheses were formulated for conducting the study.

1. There exists a relationship between the Organizational Climate, Job Satisfaction and Perceived Performance with the profile factors.

2. There exist an intra and inter-factor linkage between Organizational Climate, Perceived Performance and Job Satisfaction.

3. The Organizational Climate is positive and it is related with outcome variables such as Job Satisfaction and Perceived Performance in a shipbuilding unit.

4. The age, length of service of the personnel in public sector shipbuilding is high.

The reliability of the questionnaire construct is tested with Cronbach Alpha. The values for Socio-Economic, Organizational Climate, Perceived Performance and Total Variables construct were 0.678, 0.856, 0.811 and 0.757 respectively.

The profile factors are first analyzed using the measure of central tendency mean, percentages and chi-square. The mean age (41.53years) of the shipbuilding workers in a public sector is high. The male are employed in majority and females are present in maximum (32.4 per cent) in the age group 40-50 years. The caste representation is proportionate to population distribution and in both male and females. The females (57.1 per cent) with non-technical qualifications are more whereas men (67.6 per cent) are more with technical qualifications. One interesting fact in the study is some non-technical qualified persons are engaged in technical work and vice-versa. The non-nativity factor is high and the religion affinity is favorable to the major religion Hindu.

The Classification of employees" show females (57.1 per cent) are more in Staff category. Since, it is Engineering Company we find more employees in Engineering and Allied Services. The mean for length of service is high (18.1 years) and it is attributed to job security in the public sector. The promotion pattern shows disparity in comparison of males with females. The specialization distribution reveals men as more in Engineering and Allied Services whereas females are more in Administration and Medical Services.

The organizational climate is the perception of the employees. The organizational climate is the summation of the perception of the individuals towards the following factors Working Conditions, Job design, Performance Management, Compensation, Relations, Communication, Training and Development, Objectivity and Rationality, Grievance and Welfare. The organizational climate is analyzed using percentages and means. In the next step, the factors are examined for cause and effect relationship using multiple regression analysis. The factors are independent and the same is established by the collinear matrix (diagonals converge to unity). The organizational climate in the public sector shipbuilding organization is moderate (3.39). The Welfare as a factor has a high mean (3.58). The Relations (3.49), Grievance Handling (3.49) and Working Conditions (3.48) are the other factors influencing the organizational climate in high order. The least out of all the factors is Job design (2.99).

The intra-dimensional regression reveals that all the factors are influencing each other. However, Job design is isolated and the Welfare is influenced by six factors. The Welfare is given top priority in public sectors. The Relations, Training and

Development, Objectivity and Rationality and Grievance Handling are the major contributors in formation of organizational climate in the organization. However, Communication is a negative contributor.

In further analysis, organizational climate factors are regressed with the profile factors namely Age, Gender, Caste, Nature of Education, Nature of Work, Salary, Classification and Service. The Age was a major influencing factor of Organizational Climate. The Nature of Work is also important factor acting negatively on Organizational Climate factors. The Welfare is a major component in Organizational Climate, and it is positively inter-twined by Gender and negatively by Nature of Education, Nature of Work, Classification and Service.

The Perceived Performance is the perceptional opinion about own work experience at the work. The perceived performance is the self-evaluation of one"s exhibited performance related to behavior at work. The data on perceived performance is first examined by applying the mean and percentages.

The Discipline as a factor of Perceived Performance is a major influencing factor (3.42). The Job and Planning and Execution are the other important contributors. The Individuality (2.62) is the least contributor. The intra-dimensional factors are influencing one and other positively. But, Discipline is not influenced by any other factor. Therefore, Discipline is independent and correlates directly with perceived performance. The Perceived Performance as a factor has a moderate mean (3.14).

On regression of Perceived Performance factors step by step, we find that Discipline as dependent variable is not influenced by any other Perceived Performance factors.

The Job is an important factor affecting Guidance and Counseling, Planning and Execution and Individuality. Further, Job is influenced by majority of the factors.

The Perceived Performance factors are regressed with profile factors in the next stage. The regression of Perceived Performance factors on profile factors does not show any positive influence on each of the factor except for Classification on Planning and Execution and Salary on Individuality.

The affect of regression of Organizational Climate factors on Perceived Performance factors was examined step by step. The Communication was influencing Job negatively. Further, four of the Organizational Climate factors namely, Compensation, Relations, Objectivity and Rationality were influencing positively or negatively. The Performance Management, Relations and Welfare are effectively influencing Discipline.

The Job Satisfaction has a moderately high mean (3.82). The inter-factor multiple regression analysis shows that the influence of Job Satisfaction on profile factors is negative. The Job Satisfaction is negatively associated with Nature of Education and Nature of Work. The multiple regression of Job Satisfaction on Perceived Performance factors was carried out in the next step. Among the Perceived Performance factors only Discipline was found to be influencing Job Satisfaction. The same Job Satisfaction when regressed on profile factors, Caste and Service were found to be negatively influencing.

The results were cross checked with linear regression analysis by running Perceived Performance on Job Satisfaction, Organizational Climate on Job Satisfaction and

Perceived Performance on Organizational Climate. In all the above analysis the results were positively significant. The Job Satisafaction (3.82) is higher than Organizational Climate (3.39) but, Perceived Performance (3.14) is much less than Organizational Climate.

The first hypothesis was accepted as the profile factors are either positively or negatively influencing the Organizational Climate, Job Satisfaction and Perceived Performance.

The second hypothesis was accepted since the factors of Organizational Climate, Job Satisfaction and Perceived Performance are inter-twined either positively or negatively.

The third hypothesis was accepted as the Organizational Climate, Job Satisfaction and Perceived Performance are influencing each other.

The fourth hypothesis was accepted as the mean age is high and also the length of service.

The productivity which is a measure of performance is positive and improved from 27 man-hours per dead weight tonnage in 2009-10 to 45 man-hours per dead weight tonnage in 2011-12. This corroborates with the perceived performance result which is moderately high (3.14). However, the manpower decreased from 2518 to 2143 during the period. In an organization where restructuring has been made it is expected to show either positive or negative climate. But, fortunately the organizational climate is positive and implication can be seen on perceived performance and job satisfaction.

CONCLUSION:

The Hindustan Shipyard Limited has undergone organizational change due restructuring and policy changes. The Hindustan Shipyard Limited is one of the oldest in India and presently it is under the administrative control of Ministry of Defense. The unit in future will concentrate only on defense shipbuilding. As a part of transfer, pending commercial orders are being fully executed and no new commercial orders are taken up.

During the period 2009-10 to 2011-12, the capacity utilization decreased from 90 per cent to 75 per cent. However, the productivity improved due to downsizing and decrease in manpower. The Organization is an old establishment and there were no large scale recruitments in the last 10 years. Further, downsizing was done through recruitment by emergency policy, engaging contract labor and no recruitment on retirement policy. Consequently, the workforce was trimmed and the mean Age is very high in the Organization. The Welfare is a major influencing factor of Organizational Climate in the Shipbuilding unit. Further, to lesser extent Relations, Grievance Handling and Working Conditions are also influencing Organizational Climate. But, Job design is a negative factor of Organizational Climate. In public sector, social welfare is given prime importance, the same is shown in the result. The Grievance Handling and Relations are positive since the Government has accepted the two major demands of the employee's i.e. restructuring and new pay scales.

The Job design requires restructuring, it was found to be an impediment to positive climate.

The Communication has a negative connotation in Hindustan Shipyard Limited; the reason may be top down approach and style adopted by defense establishment.

The Nature of Work as profile factor is affecting organizational climate, the reason may be on use of workforce with technical qualifications on non-technical work and vice-versa. The same was proved with job satisfaction.

Perceived Performance is moderate in Hindustan Shipyard Limited, the discipline as a factor is the major contributor. But surprisingly discipline was not significant with any of the other factors of perceived performance. The Job factor of perceived performance is next major contributor and is significant with other factors. The Individuality is the least contributor.

In Public Sector, human resource practices and procedures regulate the discipline. The lack of individuality in the organization may be due to dependability for work and inconsistencies with skill sets. The job satisfaction is also moderate in Hindustan Shipyard Limited. Being a public sector unit, time bound promotion, internal recruitment, elaborate training and development to overcome training deficiencies are practiced in Hindustan Shipyard Limited. Overall the perceived performance is less than the organizational climate, and job satisfaction is higher than both perceived performance and organizational climate.

But, in future some more studies on larger scale are required in establishments where administrative controls are transferred as a part of restructuring strategy.

SUGGESTIONS:

The Hindustan Shipyard Limited requires restructuring of the workforce, new blood in the form of fresh recruitment are to be inducted to bring down the mean age of the workforce.

The Welfare is the major retainer of the workforce, therefore, this area may be further strengthened with modern amenities and other requirements to suit the present generation.

The Communication system in the organization is required to be modified, modern methods may be utilized, further, it was found integrated modern communication system on a common platform is lacking in the organization. Therefore, enterprises resource planning models may be utilized not just for manufacturing but for employee communication and storing employment related information. The SAP and other software may be used for integrating the functional systems in the organizations.

The open book policy in communication is a strategy adopted by many global organizations, the same may be implemented here.

The job analysis policy needs to be totally revamped. The Job design needs to be updated with necessary contents that directly influence the climate.

The placement policy should concentrate on matching the qualifications with the assigned work. The placing of non-technical employees in technical jobs is to be discontinued immediately

The perceived performance may be improved by enriching the Job. The manpower deployment policy is to be reviewed and qualification, nature of work is to be given due consideration in placement.

The organization structure can be made more meaningful by renaming the personnel and administration division as Human Resource Division. The training and development department may start the initiatives to educate the employees on restructuring and its purpose. The department may initiate organization development interventions to increase the awareness of the vision and mission statement as per the revised statement.

AGENDA FUTURE STUDIES:

In future, studies are required at macro and micro level where restructurings were done in the public sector units. Further, implications are to be tested for intensity, persistence and analyzed where restructuring of public undertaking is being implemented. The organizational climate is transient and changing, therefore it is be analyzed frequently to understand the organization"s ability to cope with change.

Some more studies on restructured organization will help the policy makers to understand the people's response to change.

The public – private transfers and impact on organization climate is to be probed in future. The magnitude of the study may cover much larger sample and number of units. The present study is considered at unit level, therefore in future macro level studies are required for better understanding.

The strength of the climate is a fascinating study and this study tried to estimate the strength, therefore in future more studies many be done comprehensively to understand it.

ISBN 9789810987589

Published By:

TIJ Research Publications PTE. LTD., 51, Goldhill Plaza,

Singapore www.ebk.sg | editor@ebk.sg